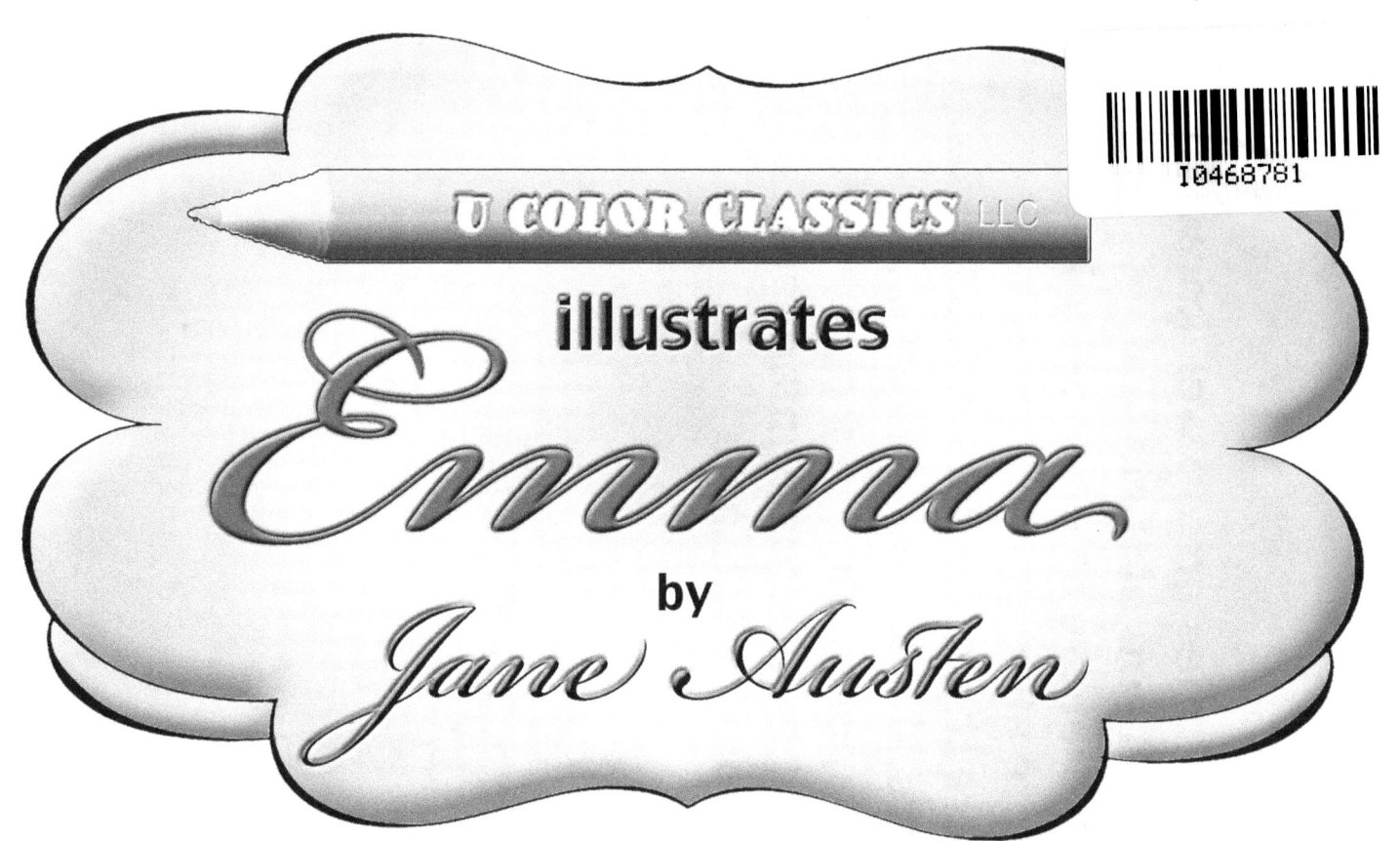

U COLOR CLASSICS LLC

illustrates

Emma

by

Jane Austen

Photography was invented nearly 200 years ago and for the first 100 years all photos were black and white. Naturally, people wanted their expensive, realistic images to be in color, so they began to add color themselves. That went on until color photography was invented. Even to this day people color black and white photos for artistic reasons.

People who tint black and white photos are called "colorists". Photos that have been tinted are described as being colorized.

Because we use photographic backgrounds, some of our pages will be quite complex. If you're not sure of what you're looking at, then just go to **ucolorclassics.com**. Each book in our series has its own page. Go to the Emma page and scroll down until you see the page you're working on. Click it and the next thing you see will be an enlarged, colorized image of that page. It should answer any questions you have.

(Cover)
The evergreen Christmas tree was a German tradition brought to England by the Royal family, which was from Germany. The first tree was introduced late in the 18th century, during the reign of King George III.

We don't adhere to Jane Austen's plots. The stories are so well known that we don't feel the need to inform you of them.

However, it's hard to resist showing details that are often overlooked. For instance, the Gypsies in this story were alive at the time when the Gypsy Caravans first appeared. They were the gaily decorated horse drawn wagons that Gypsies, or Travelers, lived and worked in.

Their music was and is much appreciated.

The two central characters in the picture of their encampment are actually Laurel and Hardy taken from their movie *The Bohemian Girl.*

U COLOR CLASSICS

LLC TM

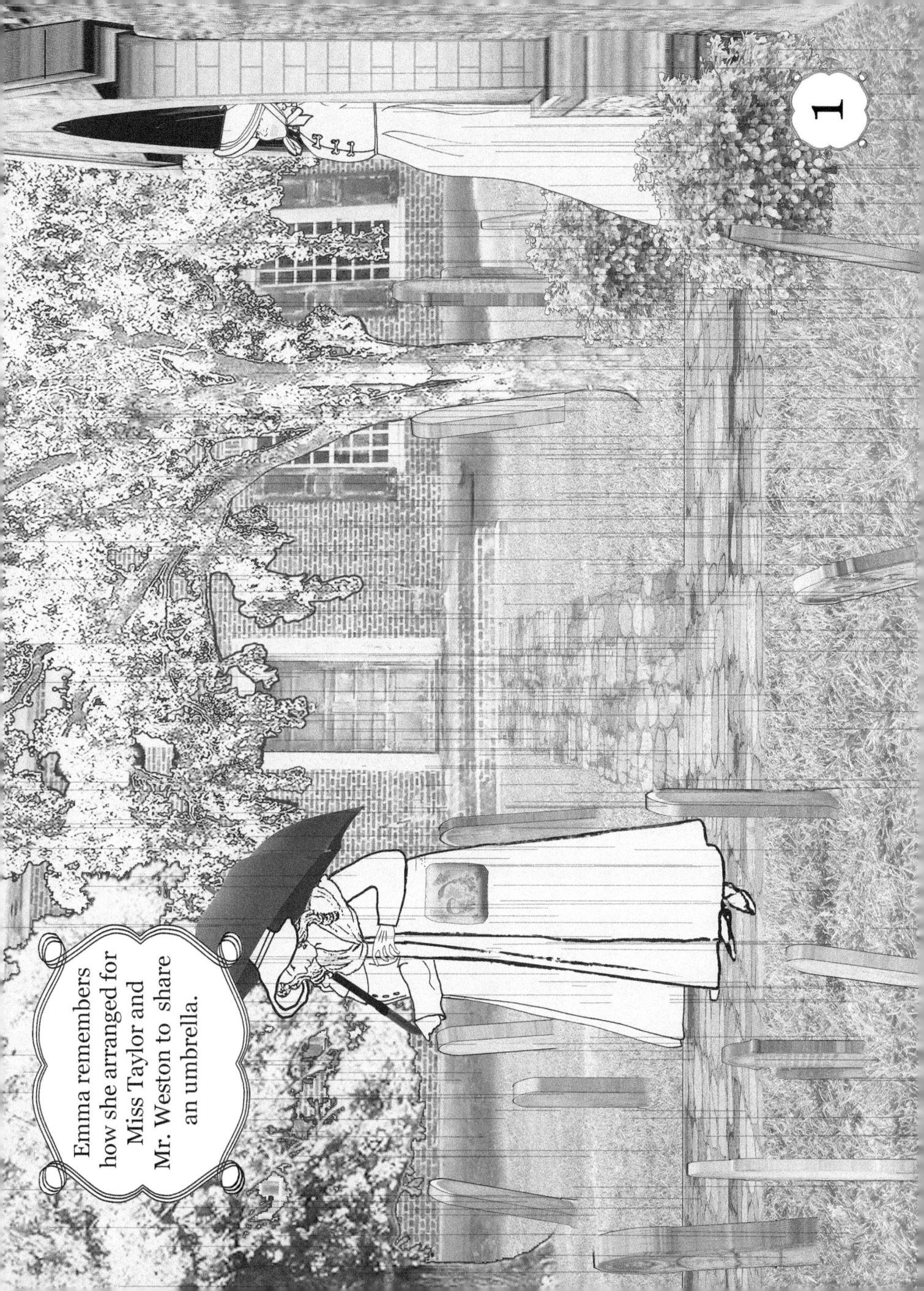

Emma remembers how she arranged for Miss Taylor and Mr. Weston to share an umbrella.

1

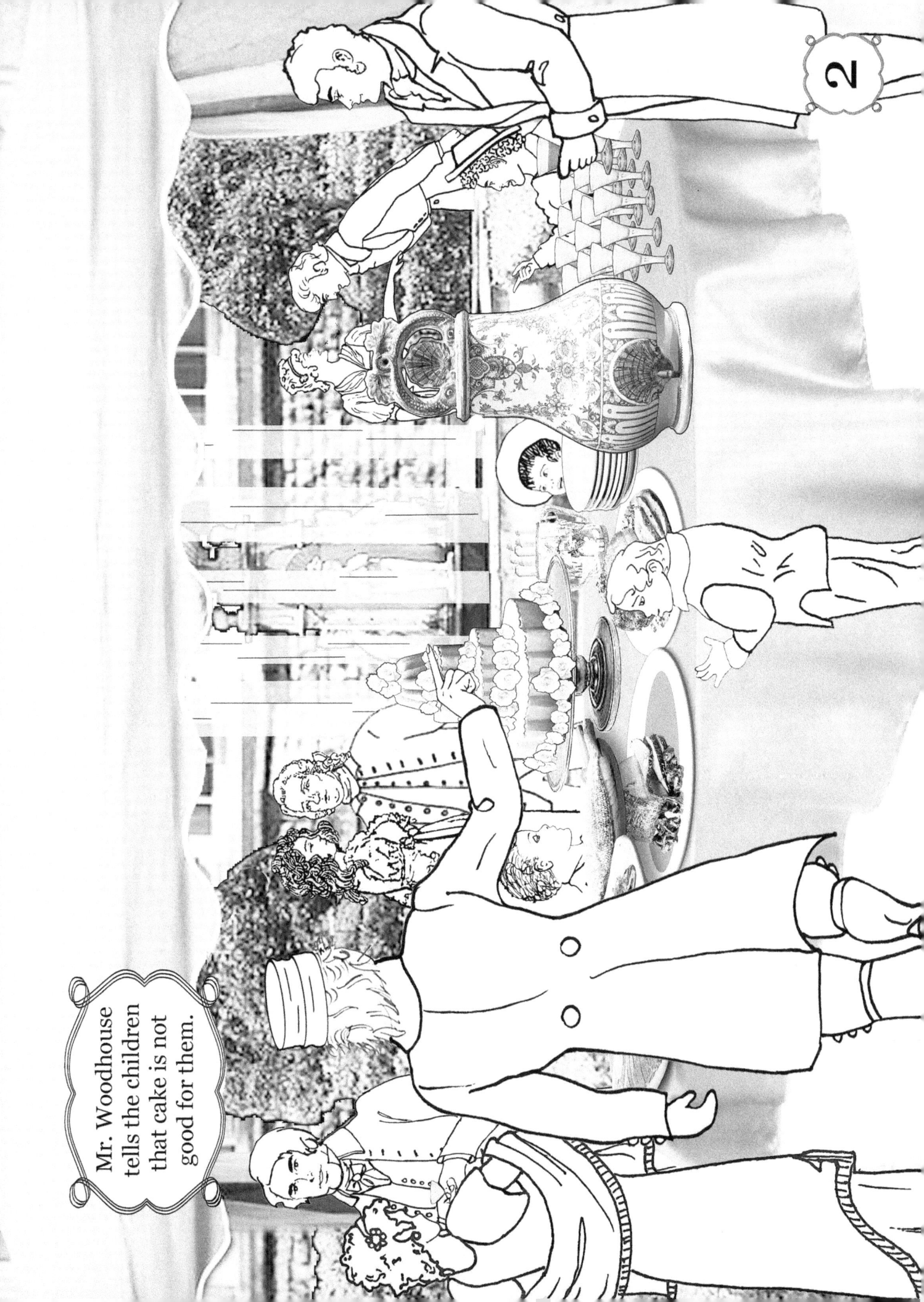

Mr. Woodhouse tells the children that cake is not good for them.

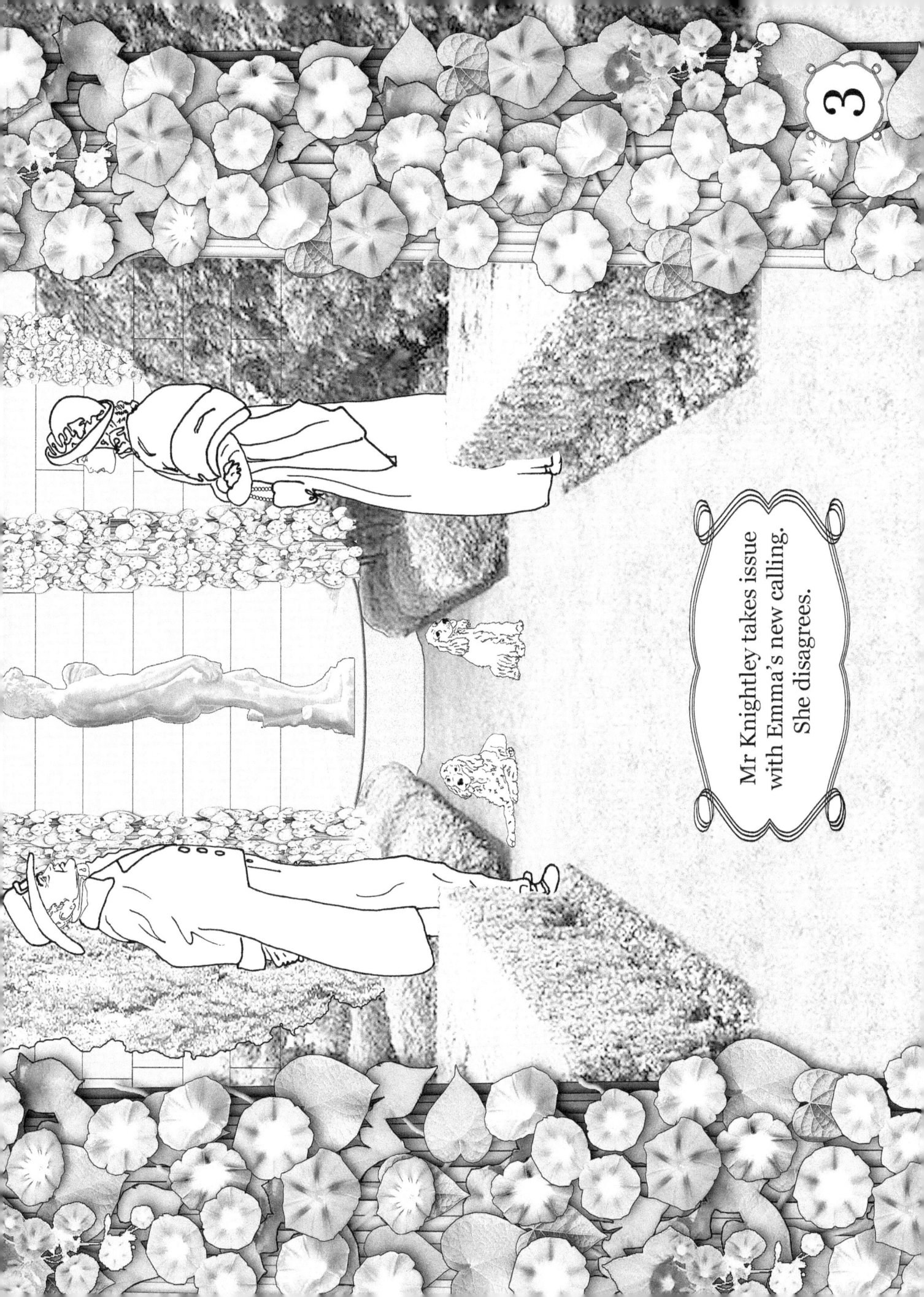

Mr Knightley takes issue with Emma's new calling. She disagrees.

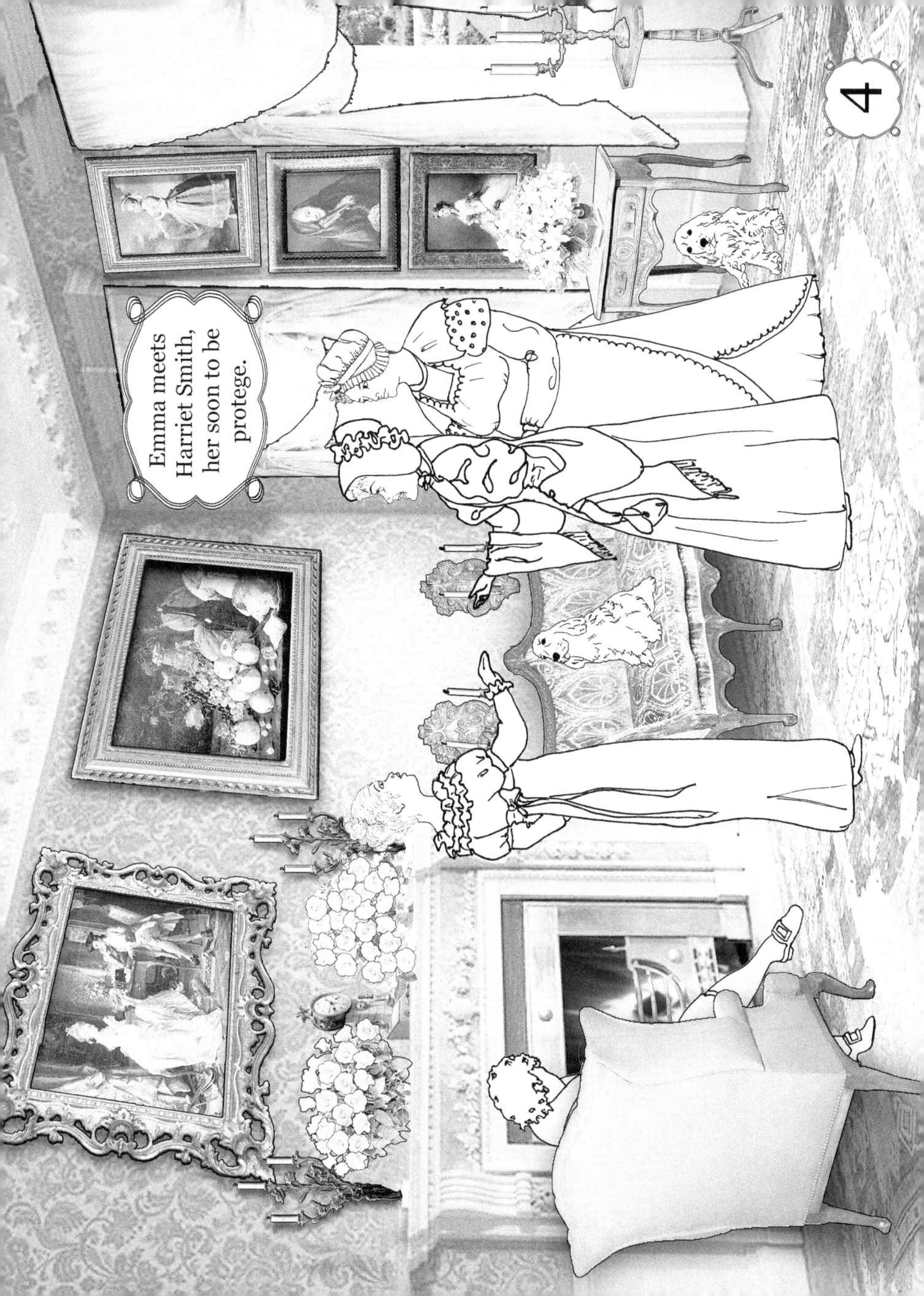

Emma meets Harriet Smith, her soon to be protege.

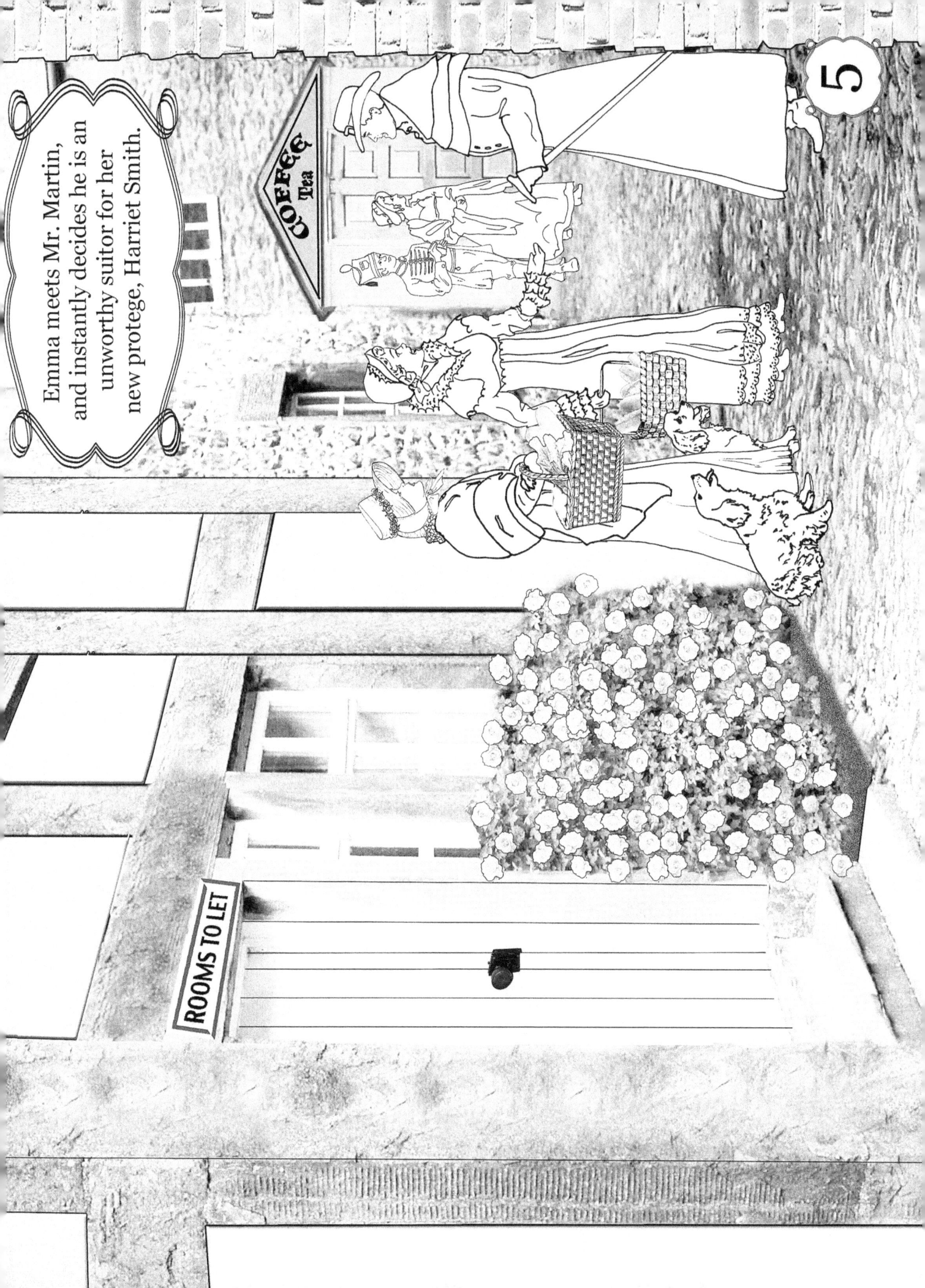

Emma meets Mr. Martin, and instantly decides he is an unworthy suitor for her new protege, Harriet Smith.

COFFEE
Tea

ROOMS TO LET

5

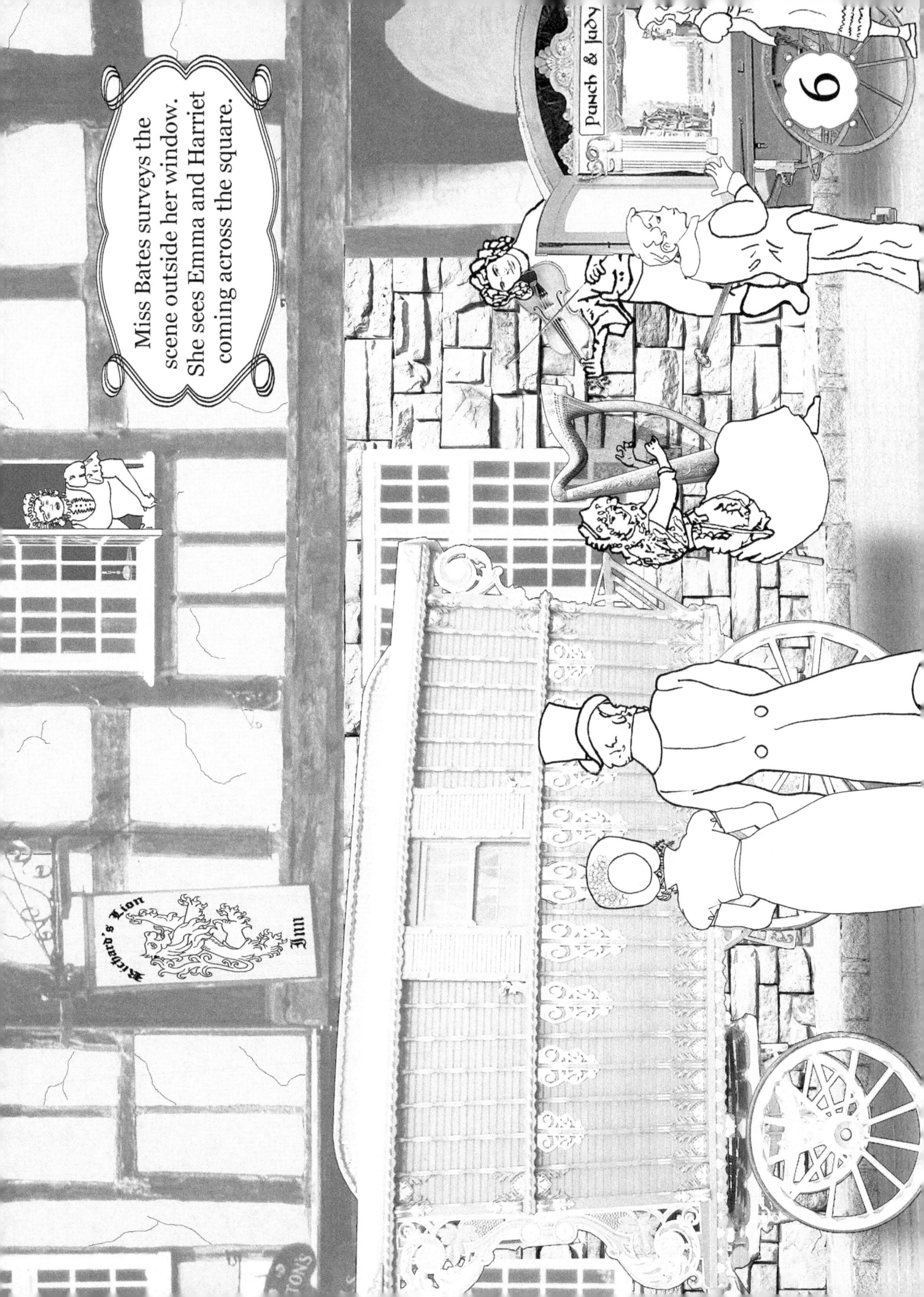

Miss Bates surveys the scene outside her window. She sees Emma and Harriet coming across the square.

Punch & Judy

Richard's Lion Inn

9

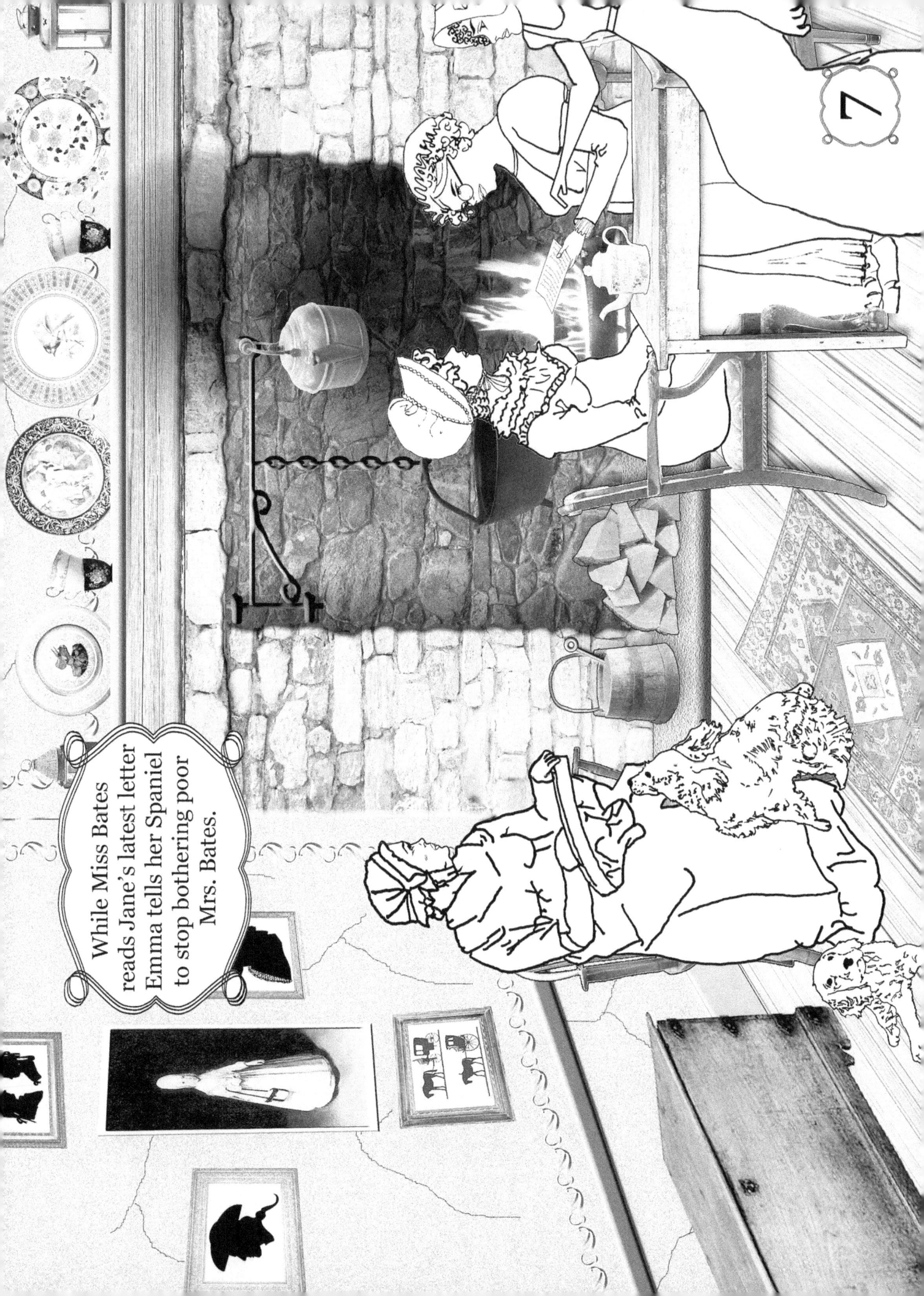

While Miss Bates reads Jane's latest letter Emma tells her Spaniel to stop bothering poor Mrs. Bates.

7

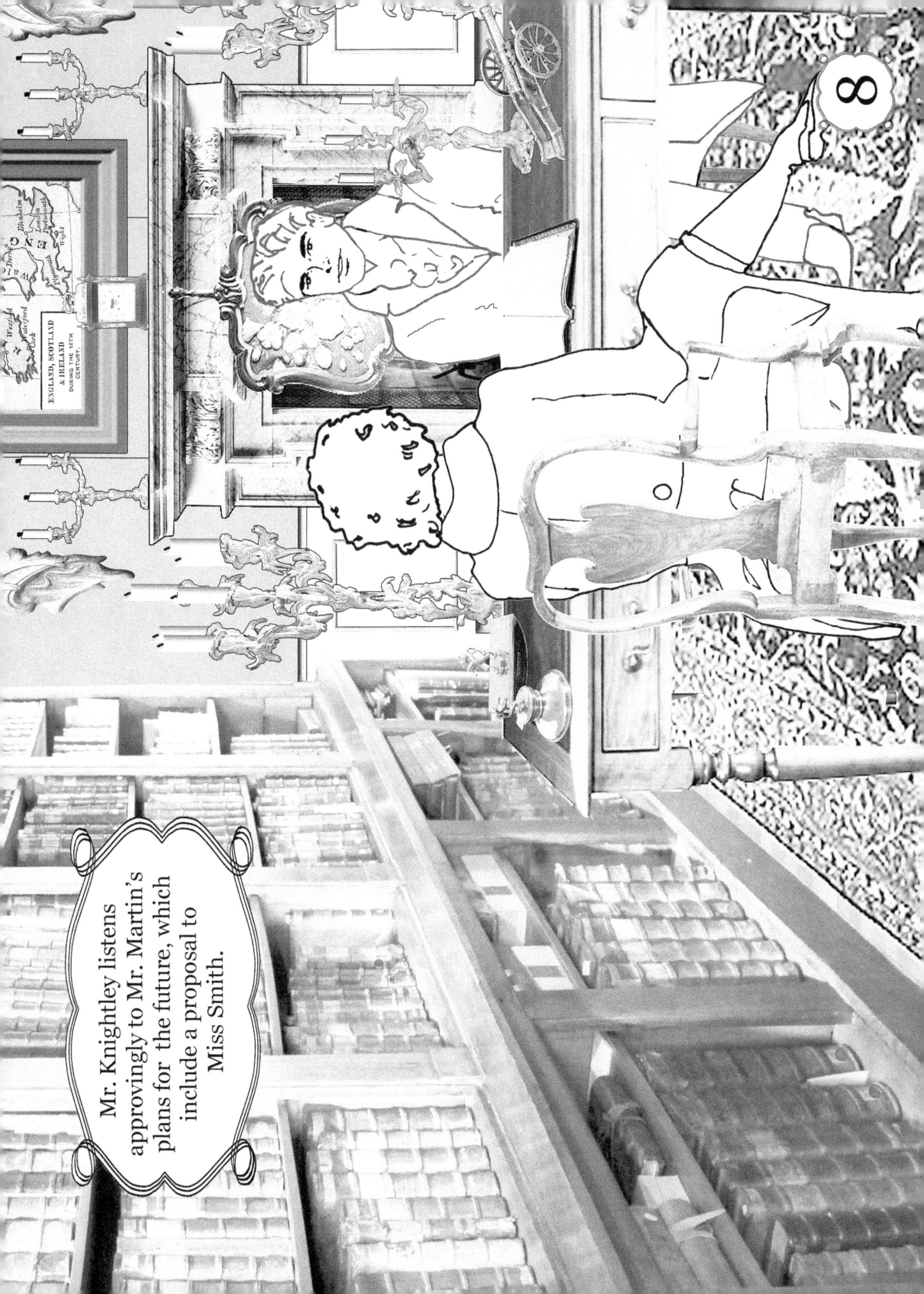

Mr. Knightley listens approvingly to Mr. Martin's plans for the future, which include a proposal to Miss Smith.

8

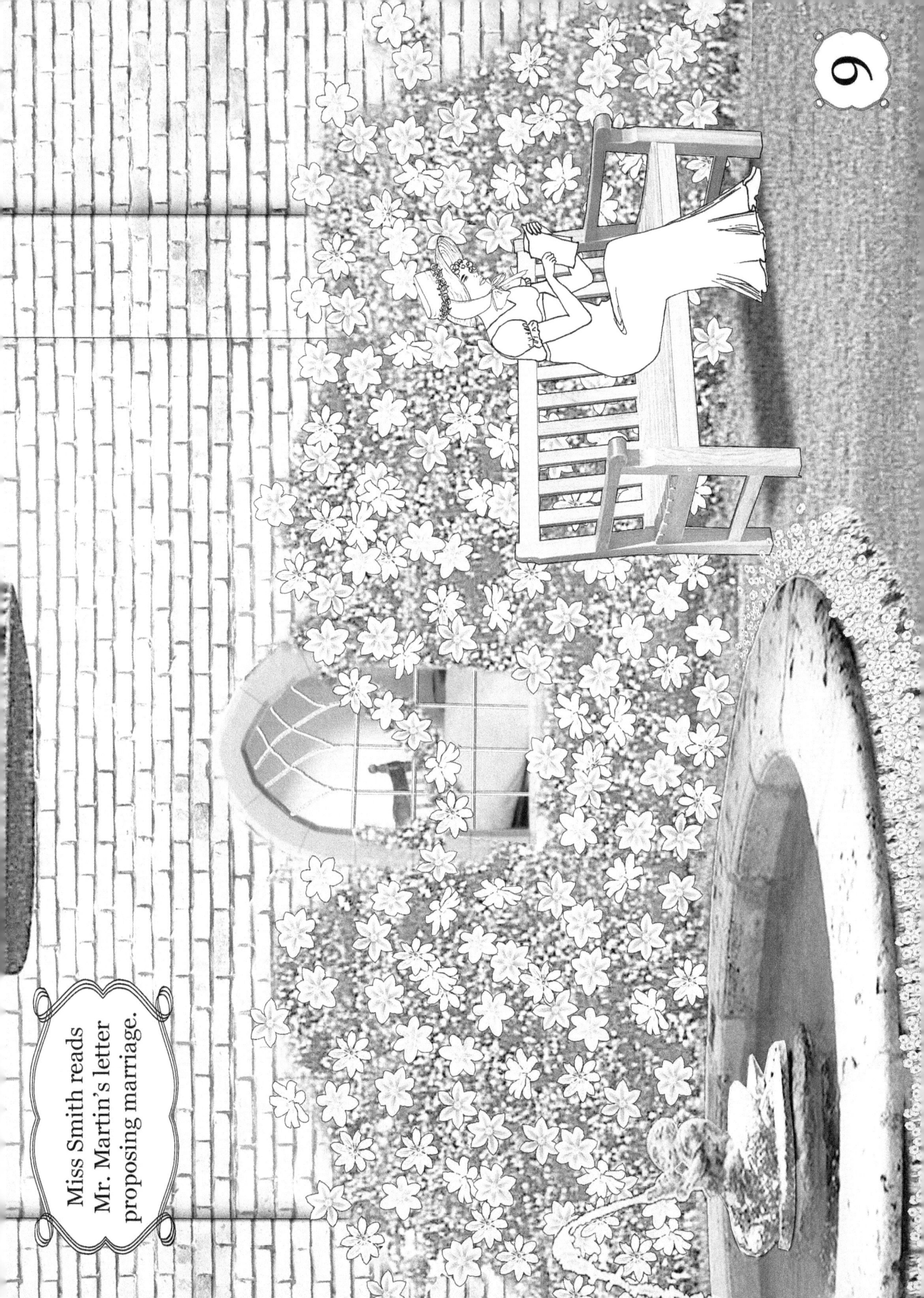

Miss Smith reads Mr. Martin's letter proposing marriage.

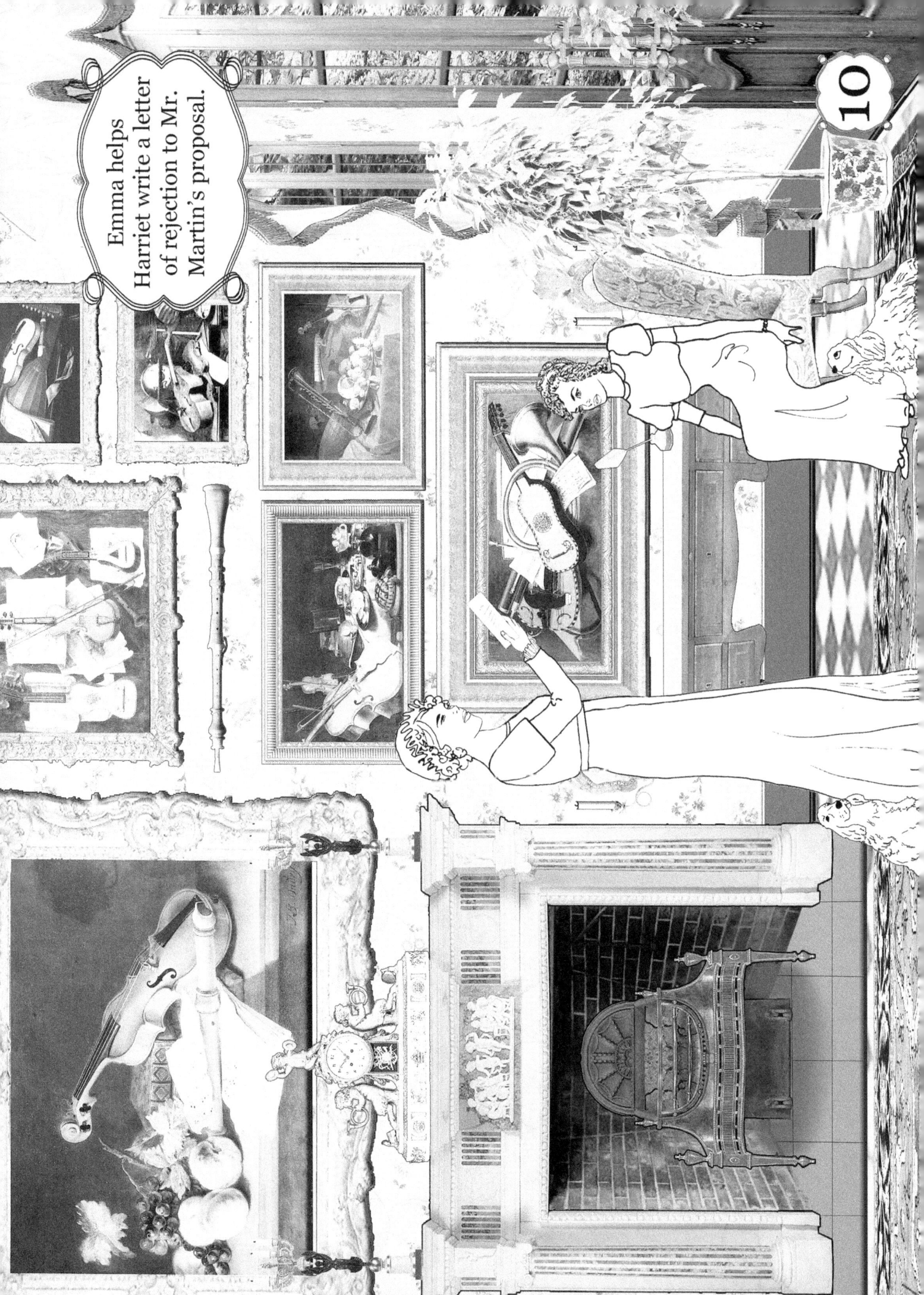

Emma helps Harriet write a letter of rejection to Mr. Martin's proposal.

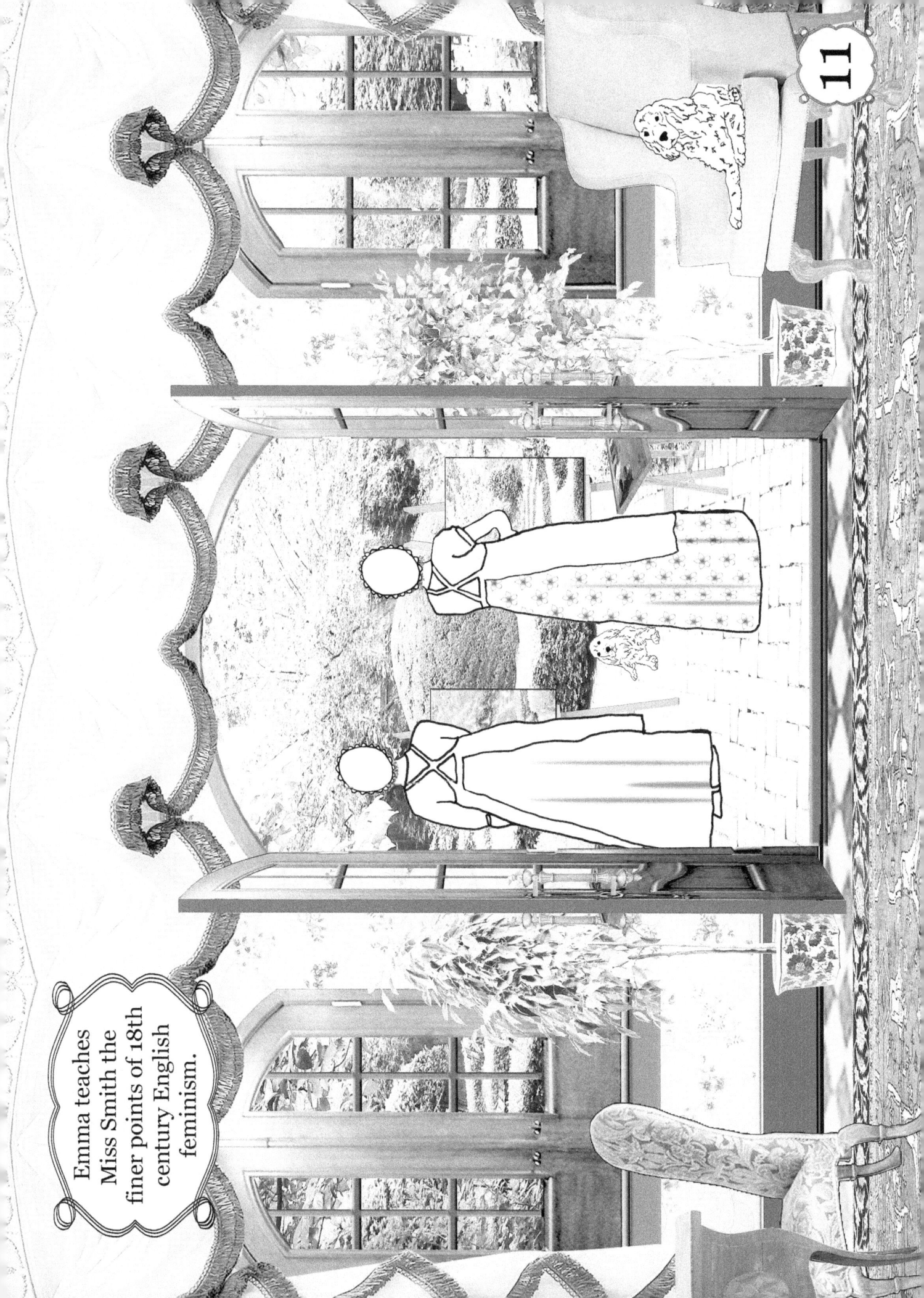

Emma teaches Miss Smith the finer points of 18th century English feminism.

11

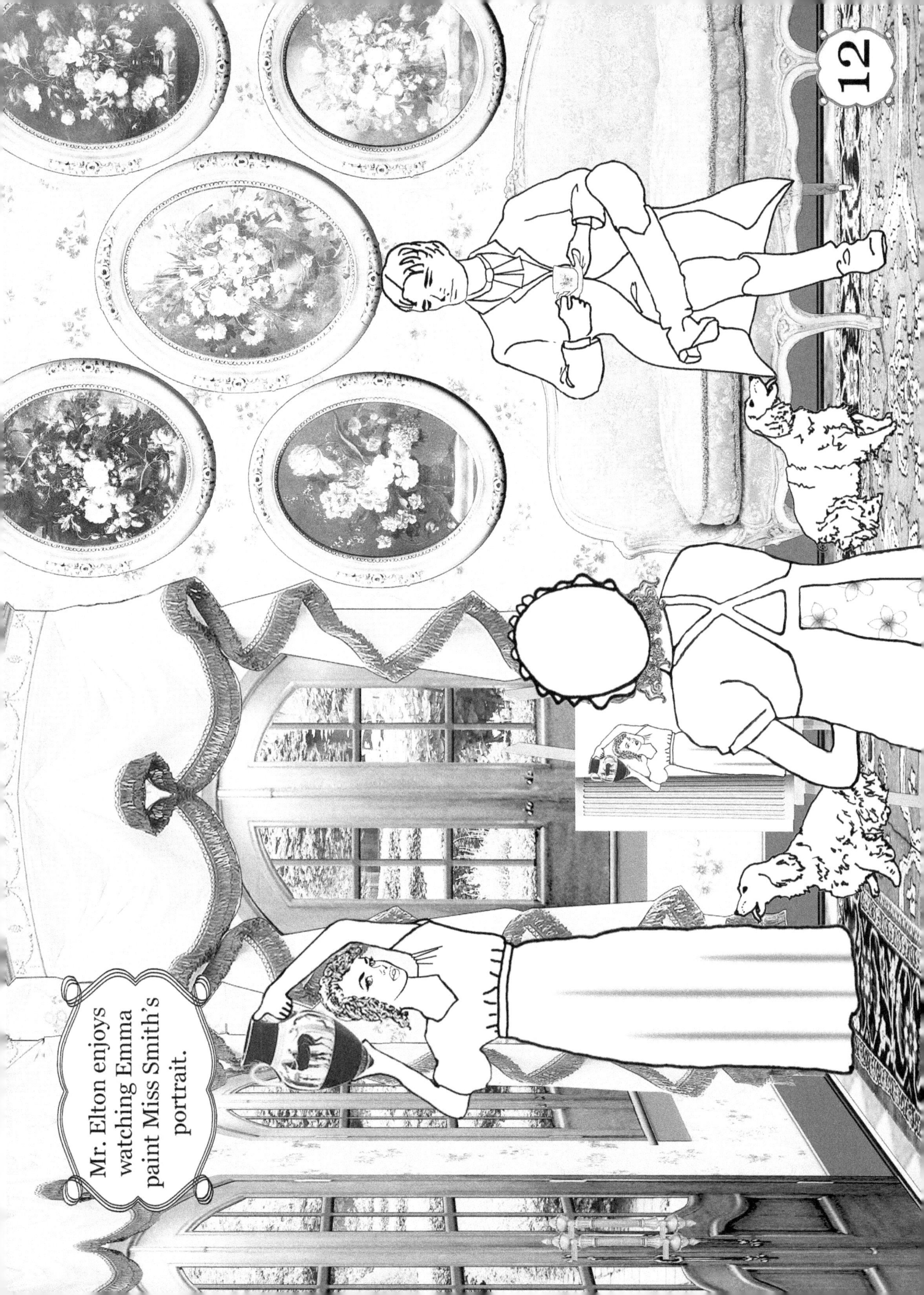

Mr. Elton enjoys watching Emma paint Miss Smith's portrait.

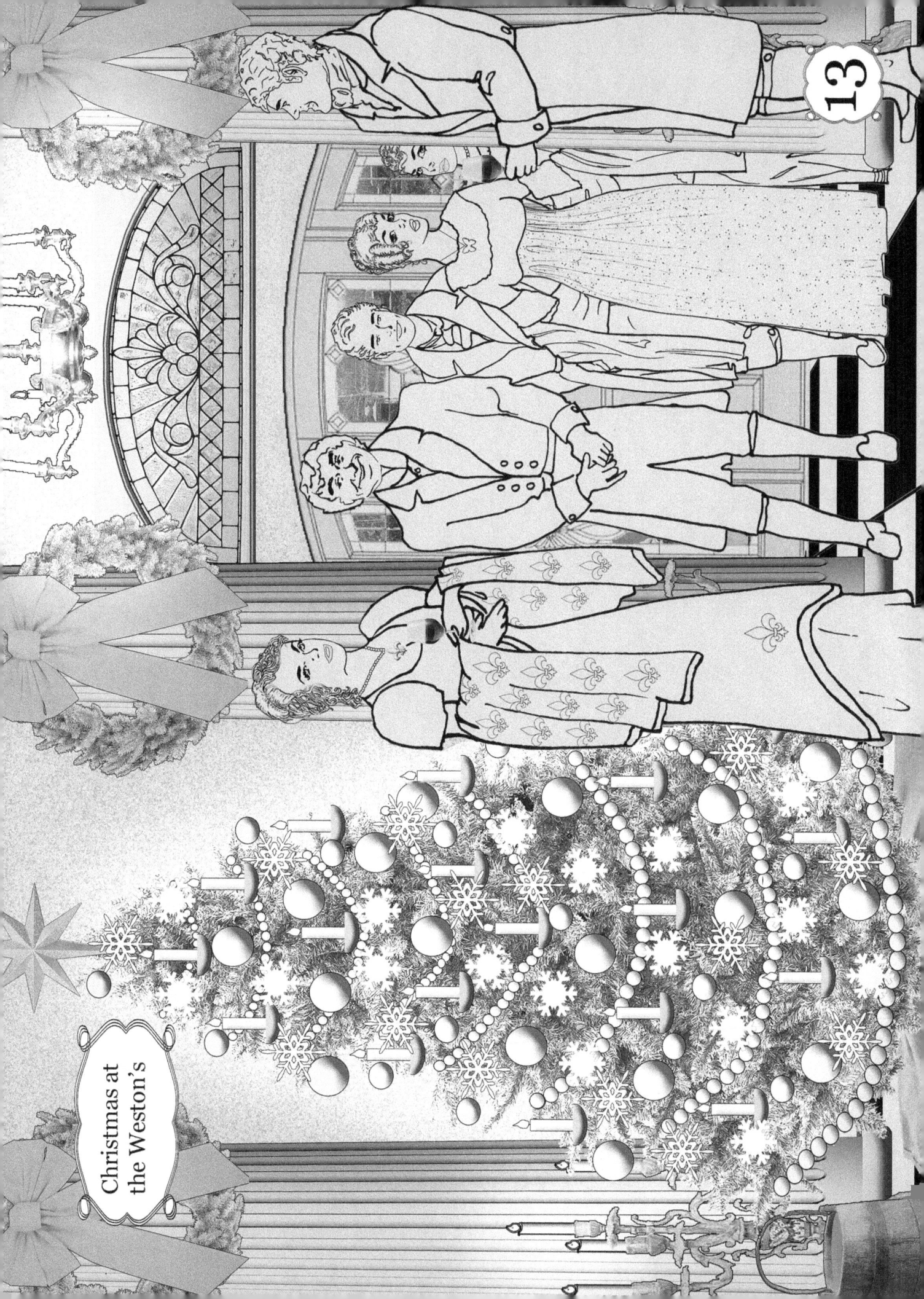

Christmas at the Weston's

13

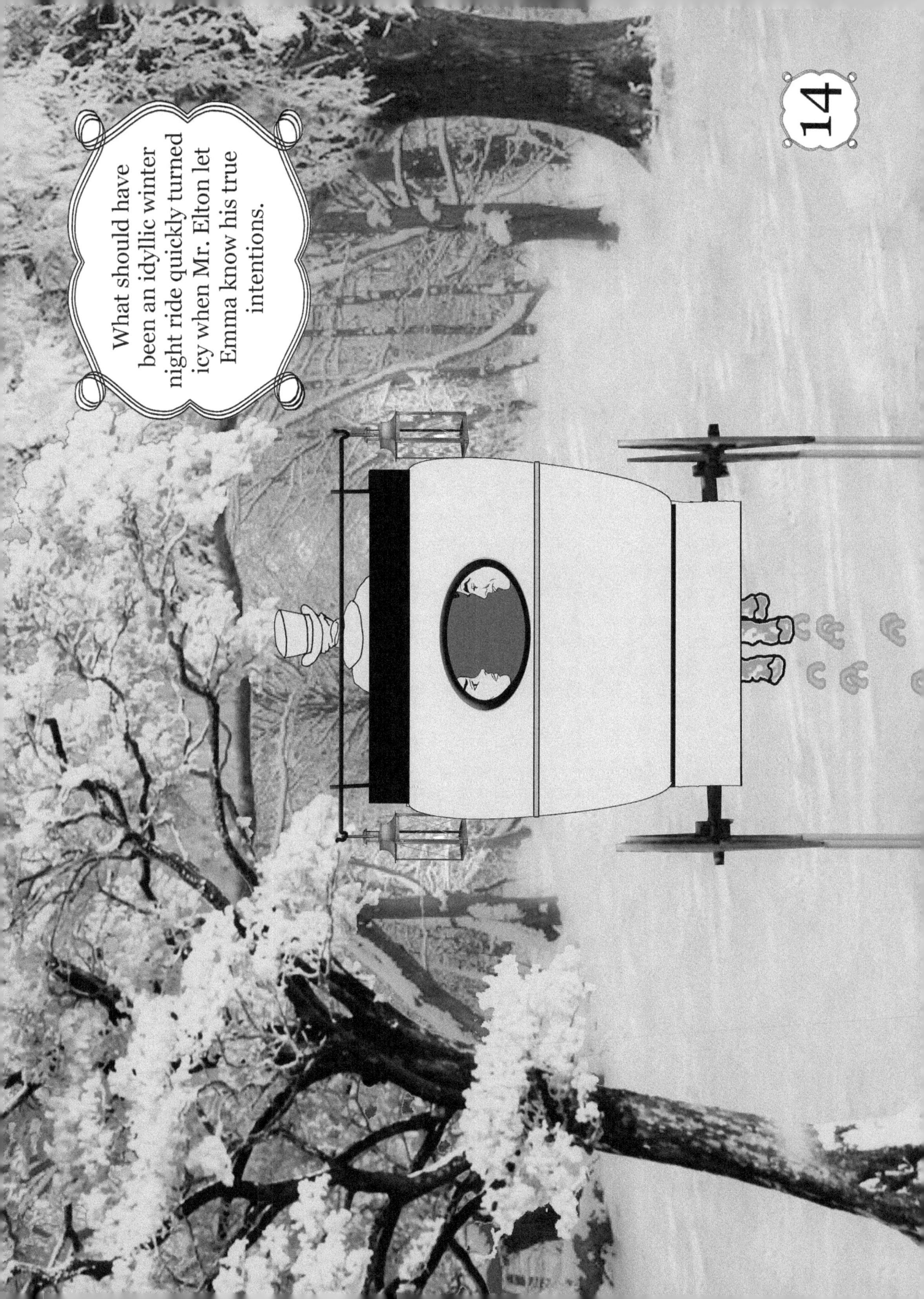

What should have been an idyllic winter night ride quickly turned icy when Mr. Elton let Emma know his true intentions.

14

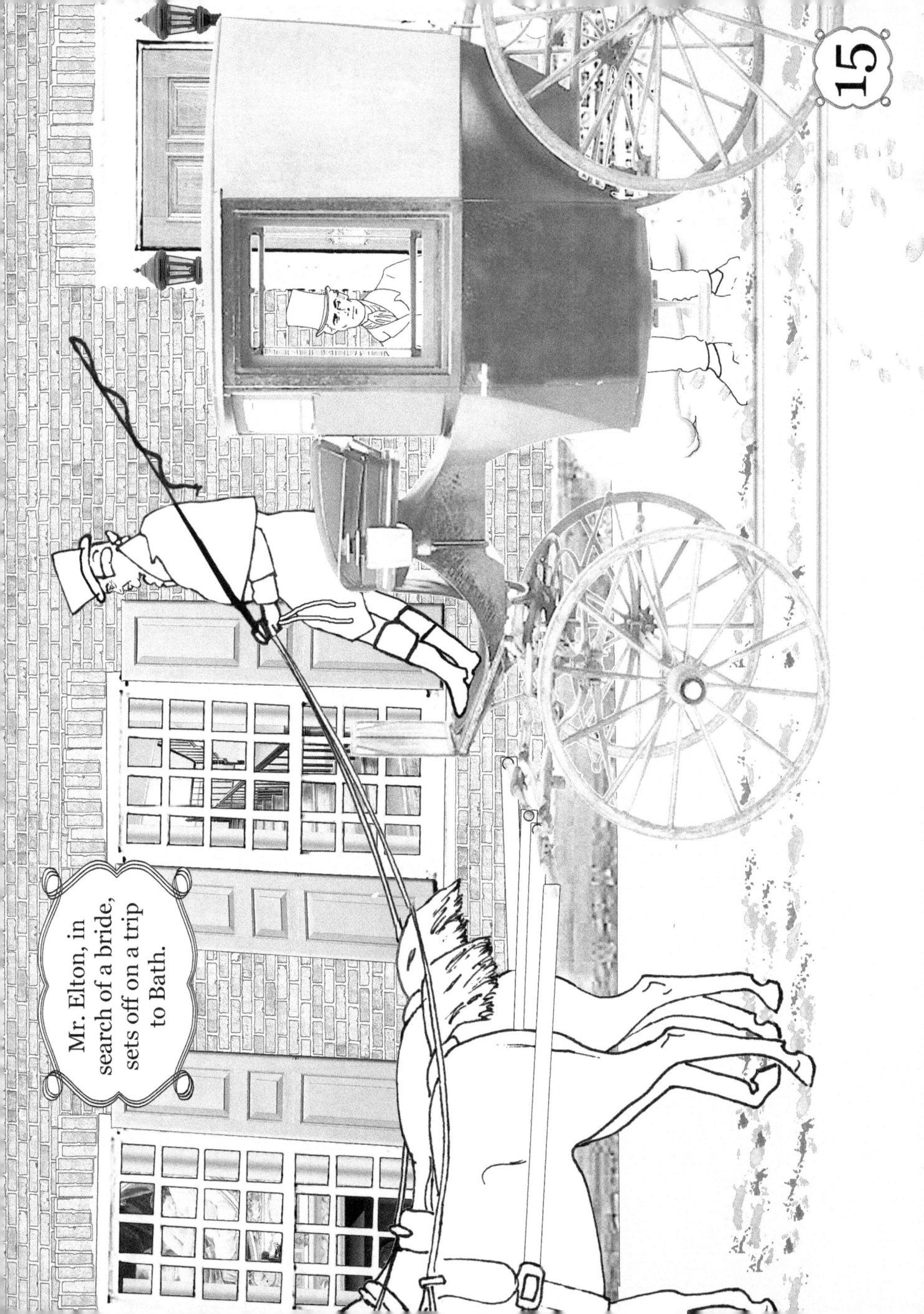

Mr. Elton, in search of a bride, sets off on a trip to Bath.

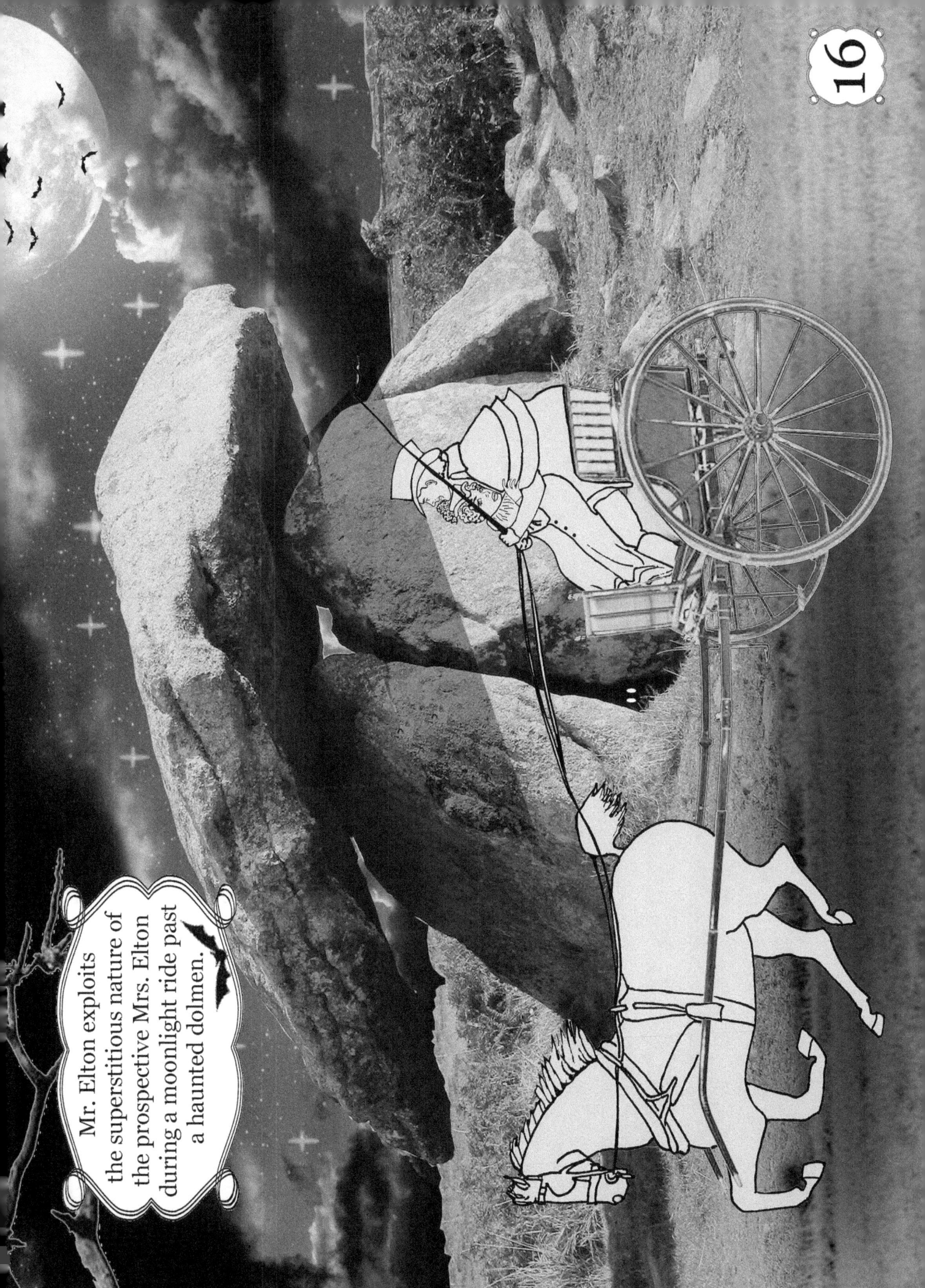

Mr. Elton exploits the superstitious nature of the prospective Mrs. Elton during a moonlight ride past a haunted dolmen.

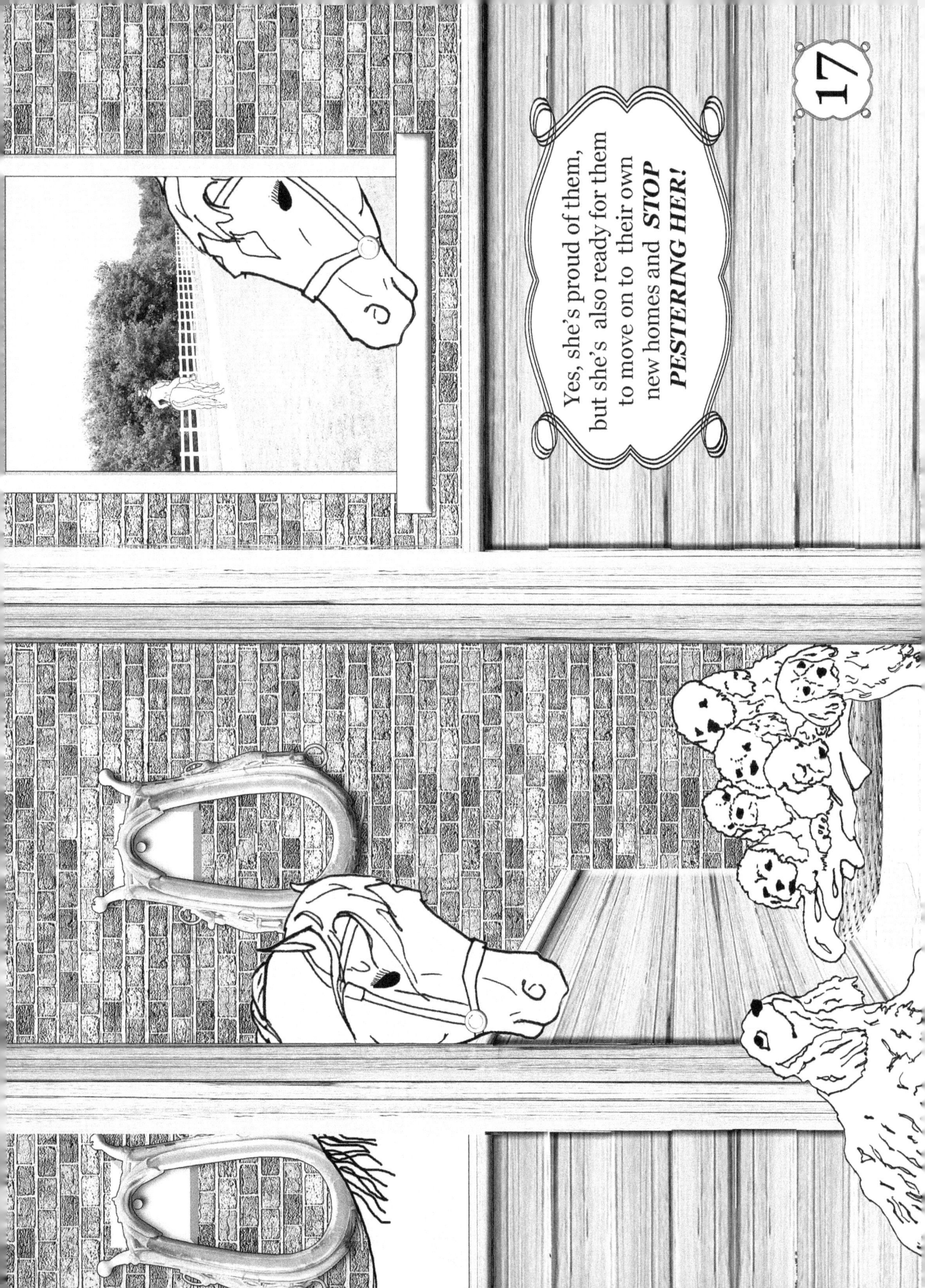

Yes, she's proud of them, but she's also ready for them to move on to their own new homes and *STOP PESTERING HER!*

17

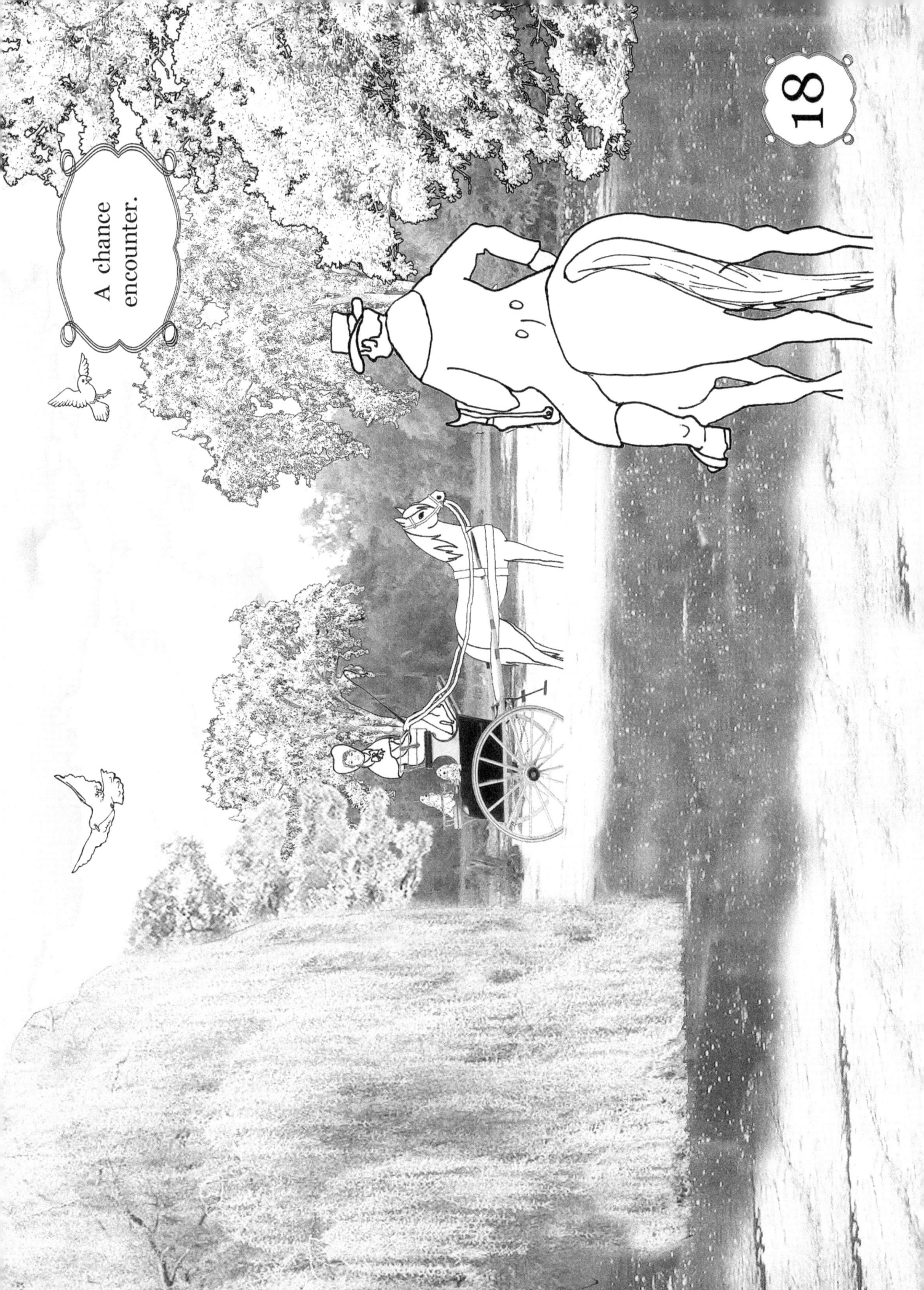

A chance encounter.

18

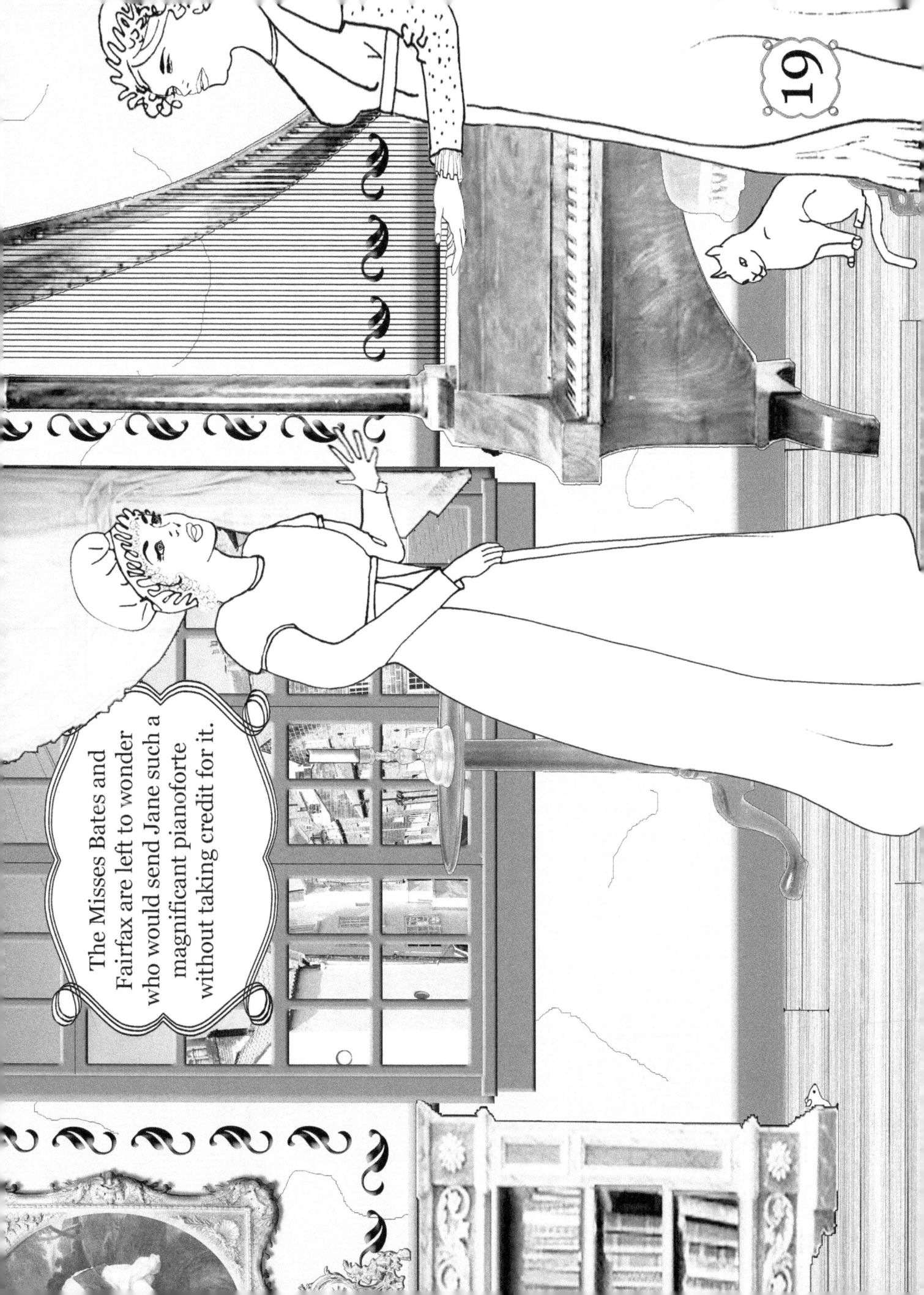

The Misses Bates and Fairfax are left to wonder who would send Jane such a magnificent pianoforte without taking credit for it.

19

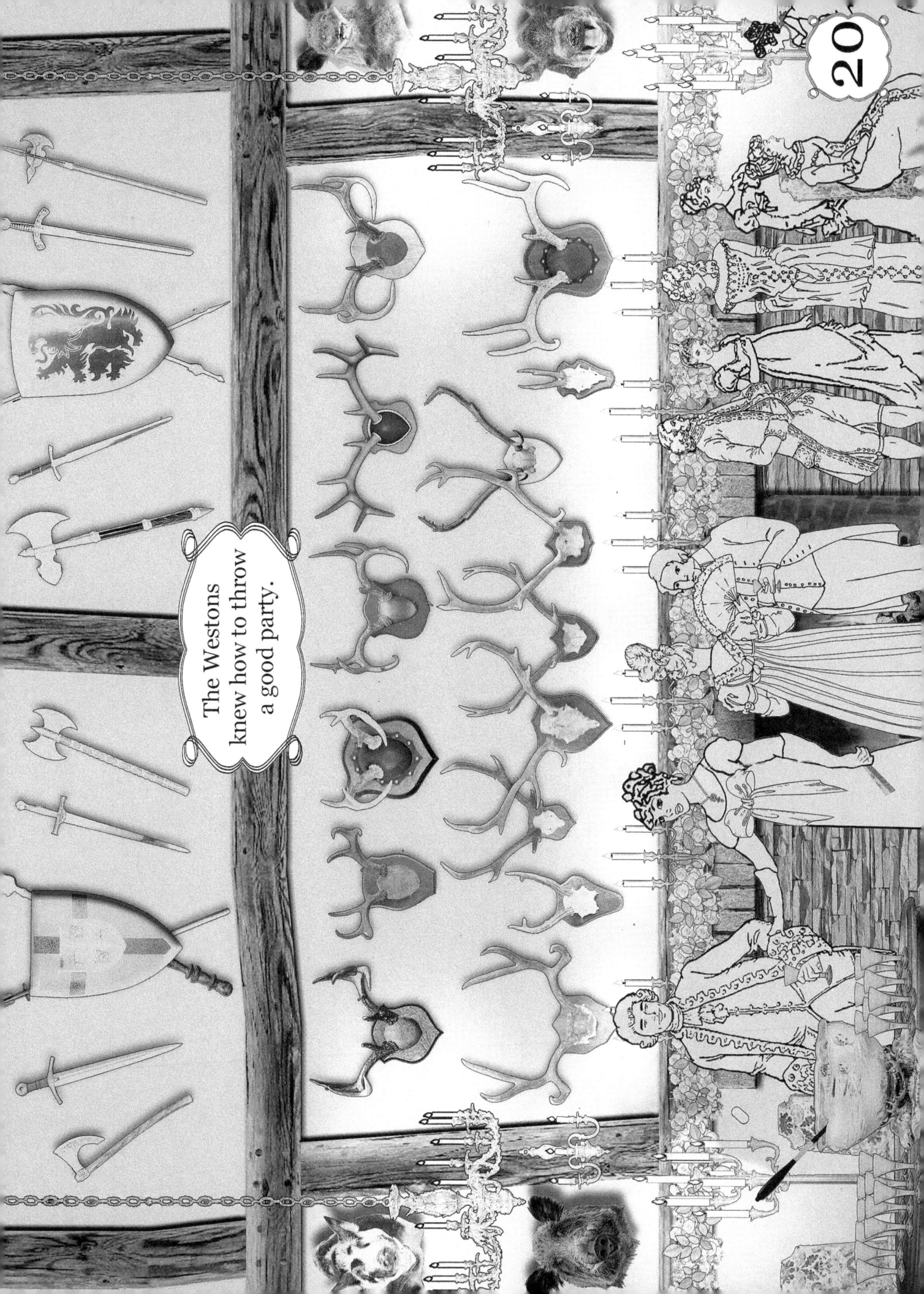

The Westons knew how to throw a good party.

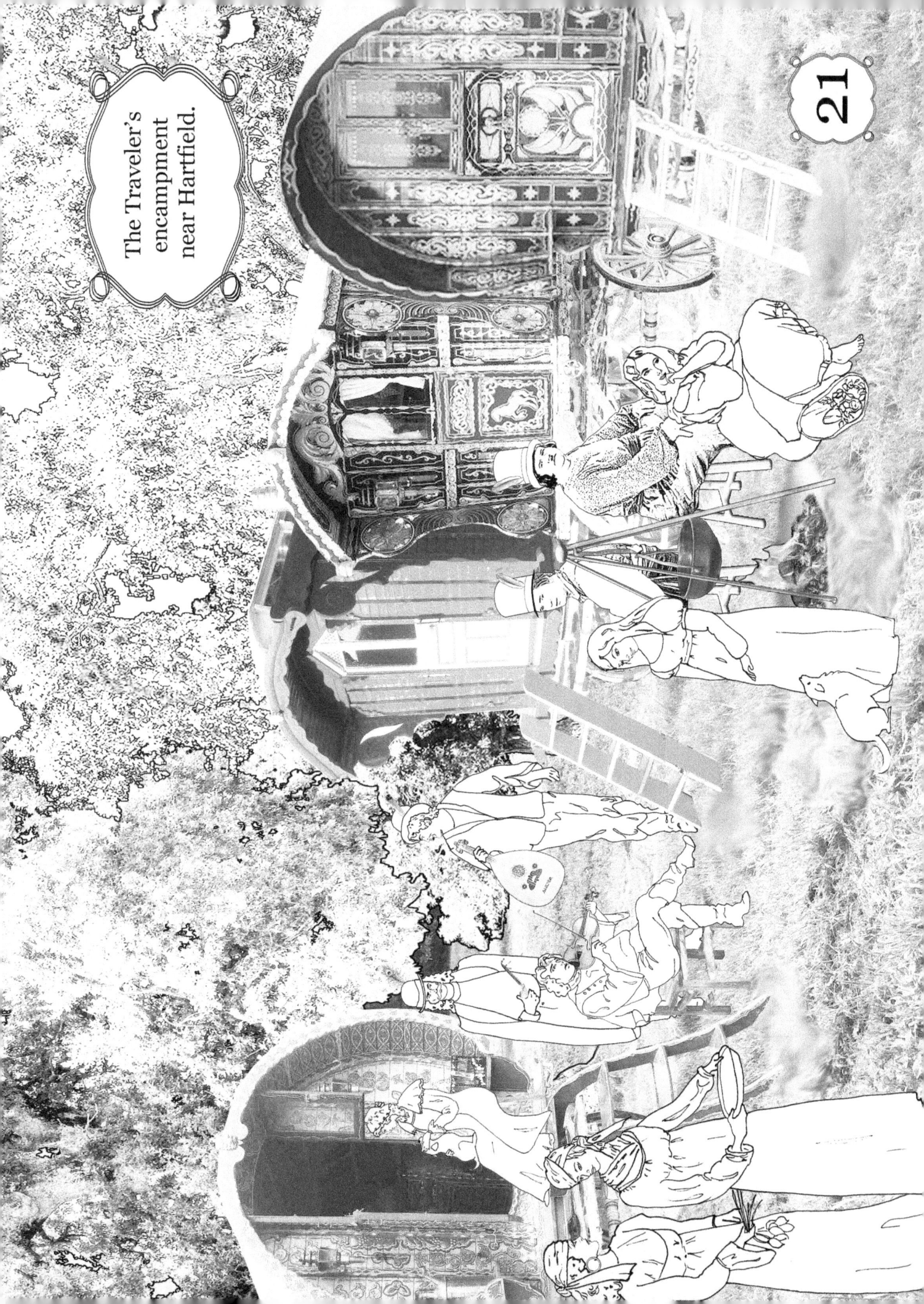

The Traveler's encampment near Hartfield.

21

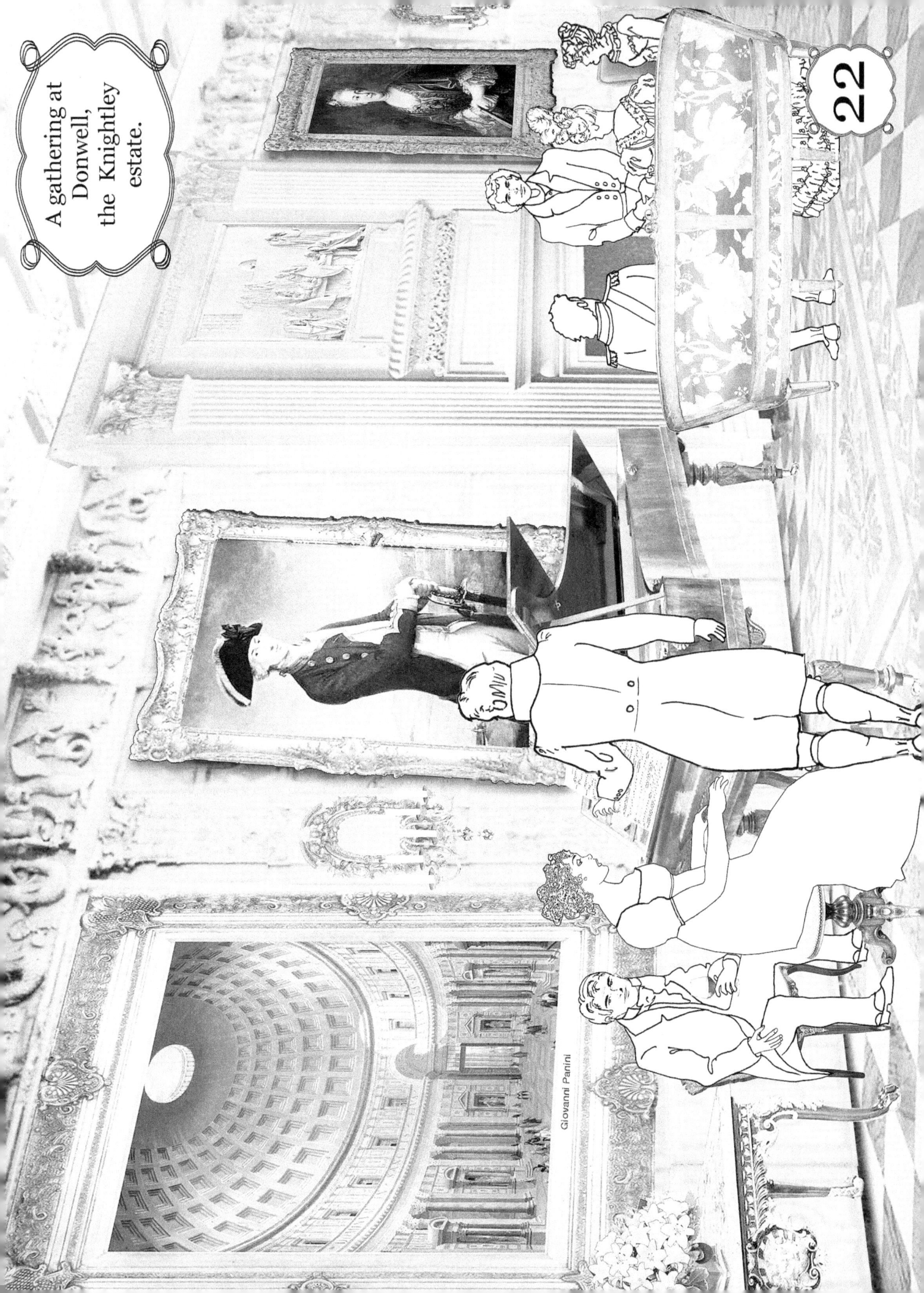

A gathering at Donwell, the Knightley estate.

Giovanni Panini

22

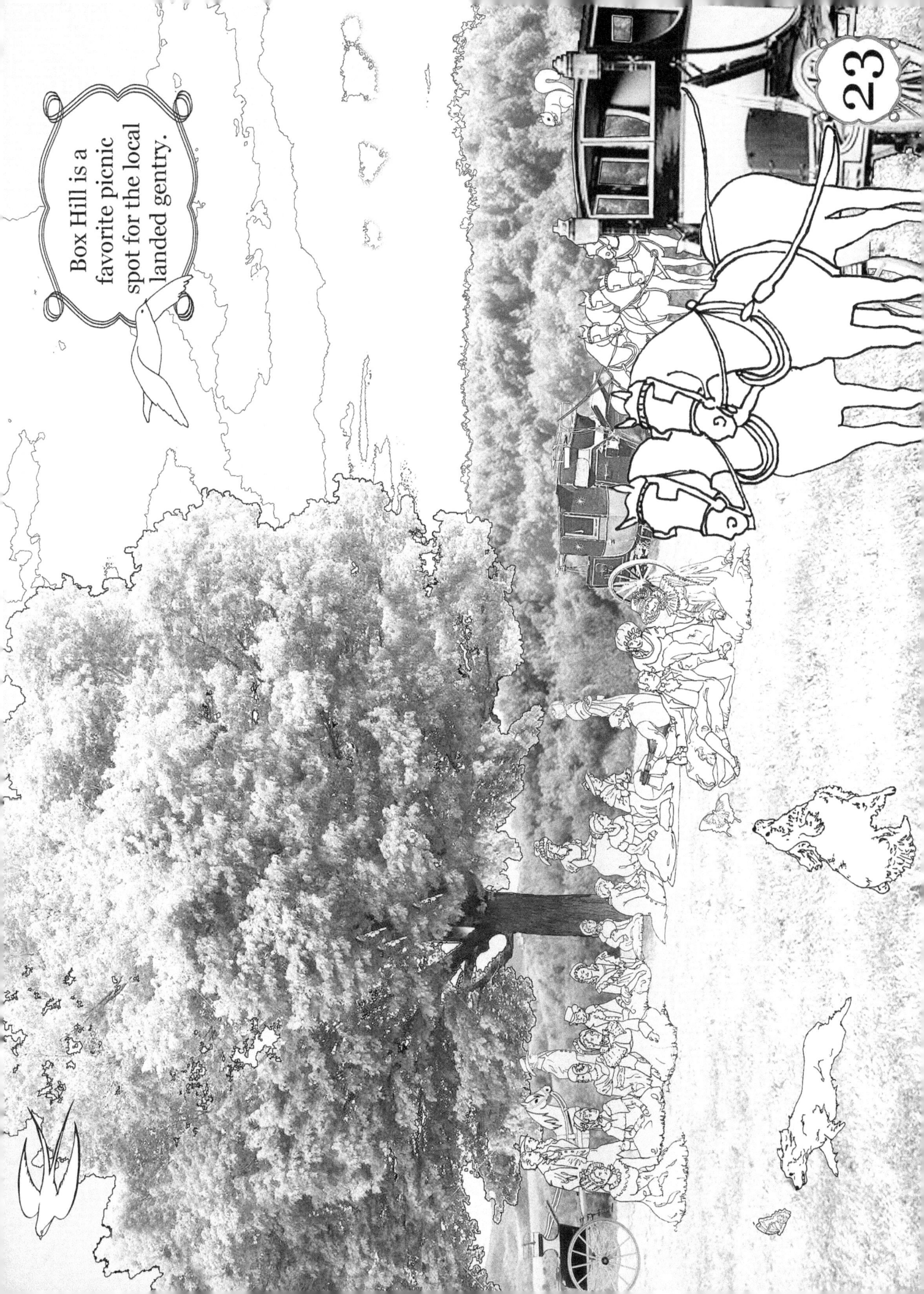

Box Hill is a favorite picnic spot for the local landed gentry.

23

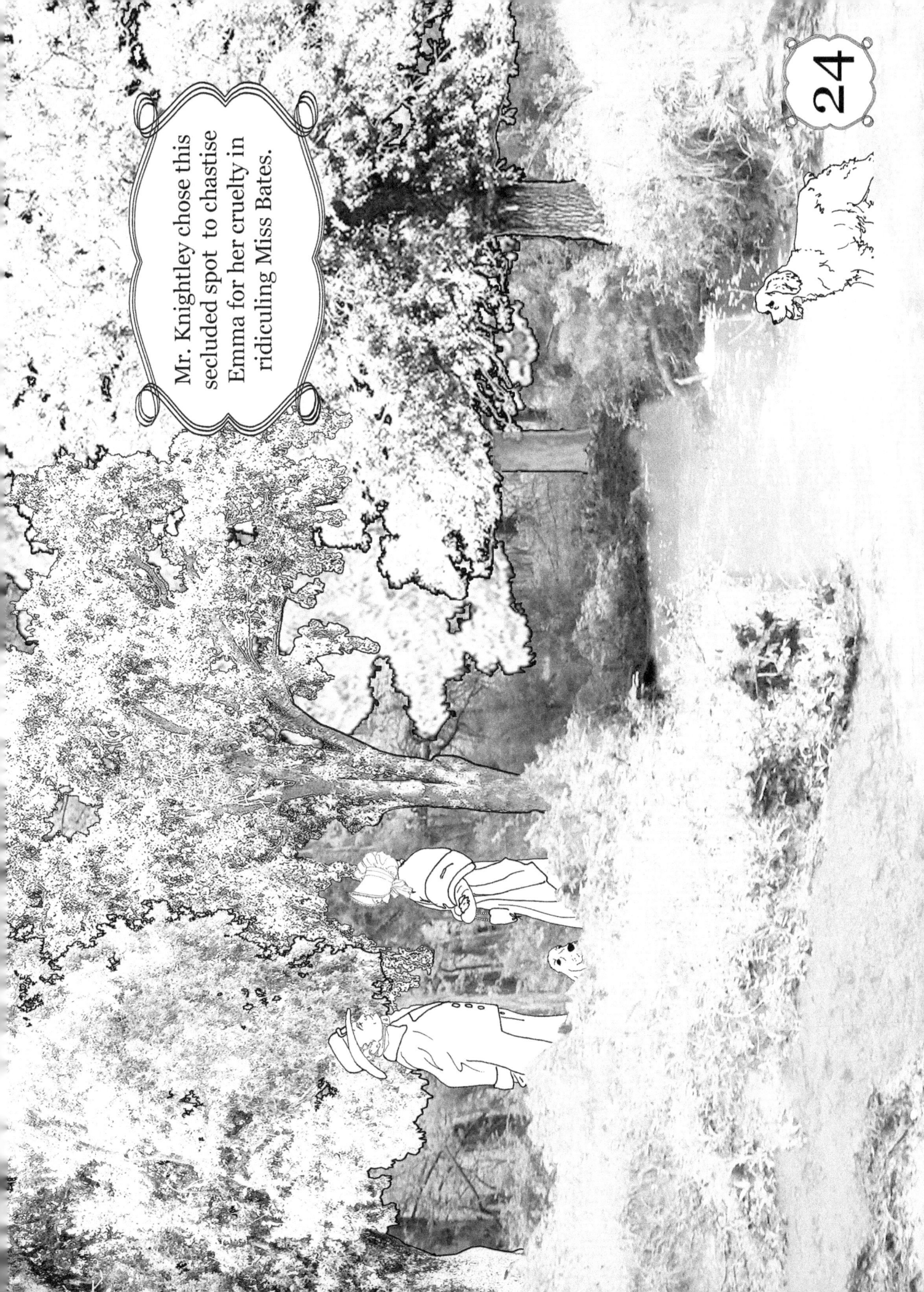

Mr. Knightley chose this secluded spot to chastise Emma for her cruelty in ridiculing Miss Bates.

24

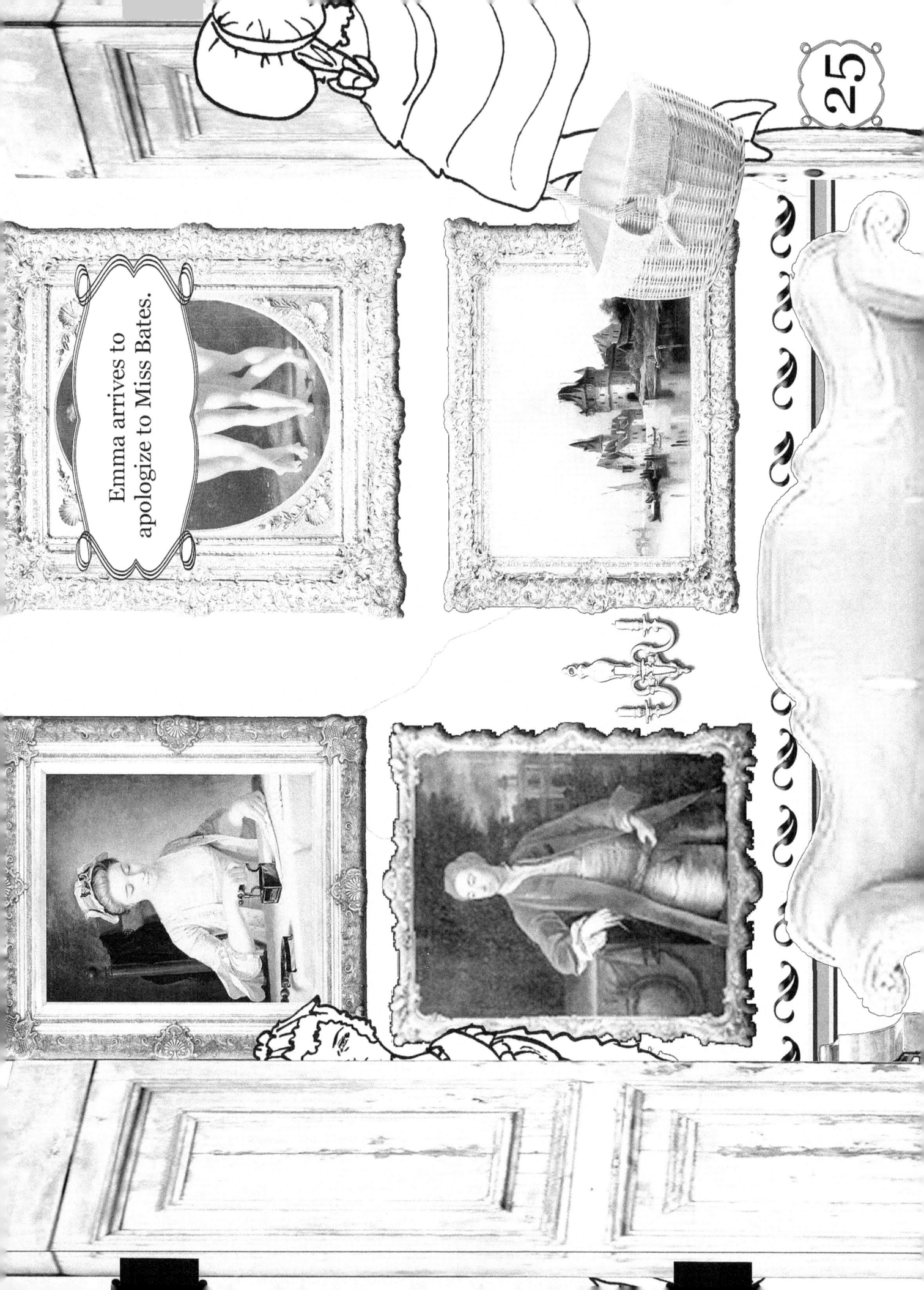

Emma arrives to apologize to Miss Bates.

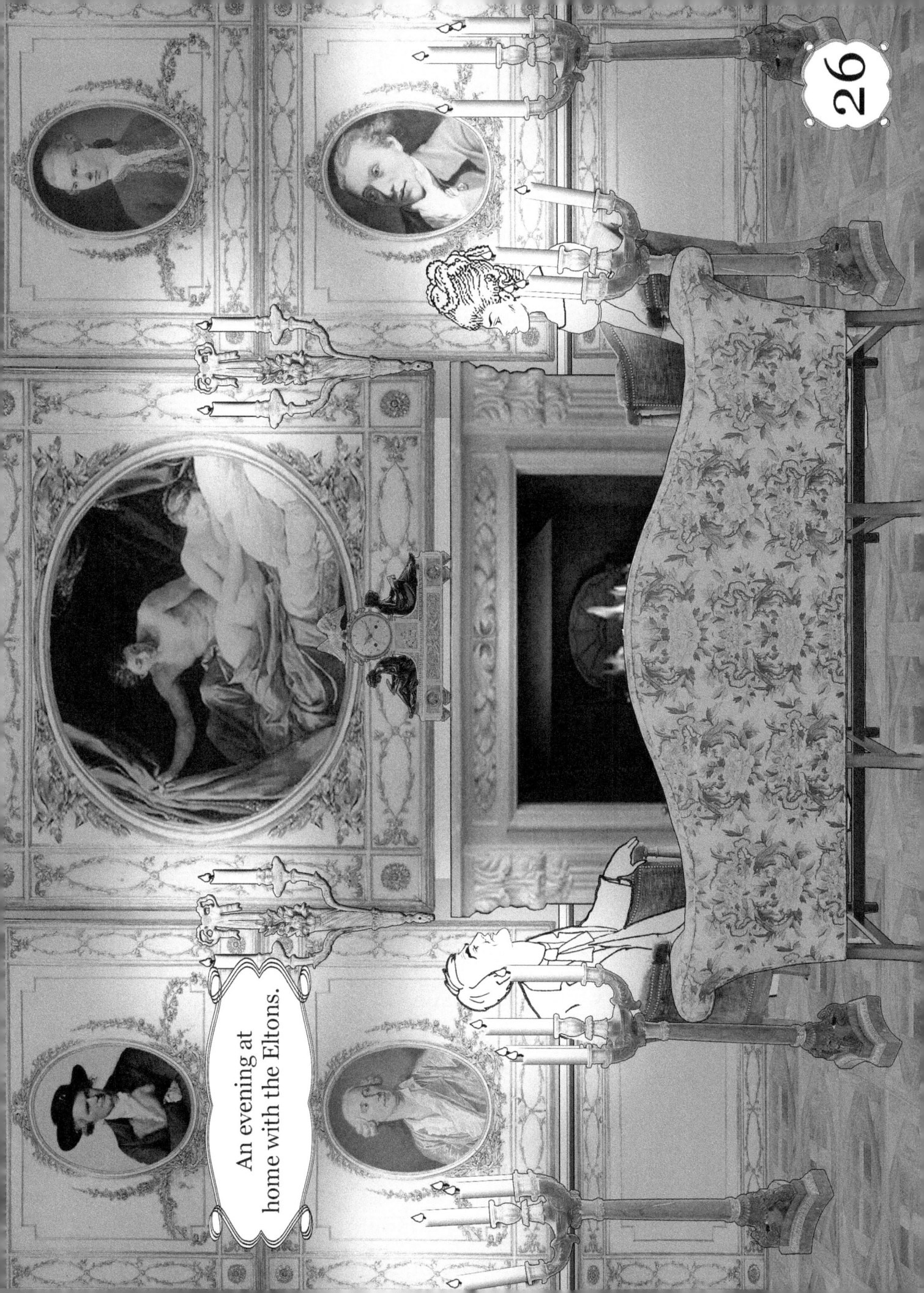

An evening at home with the Eltons.

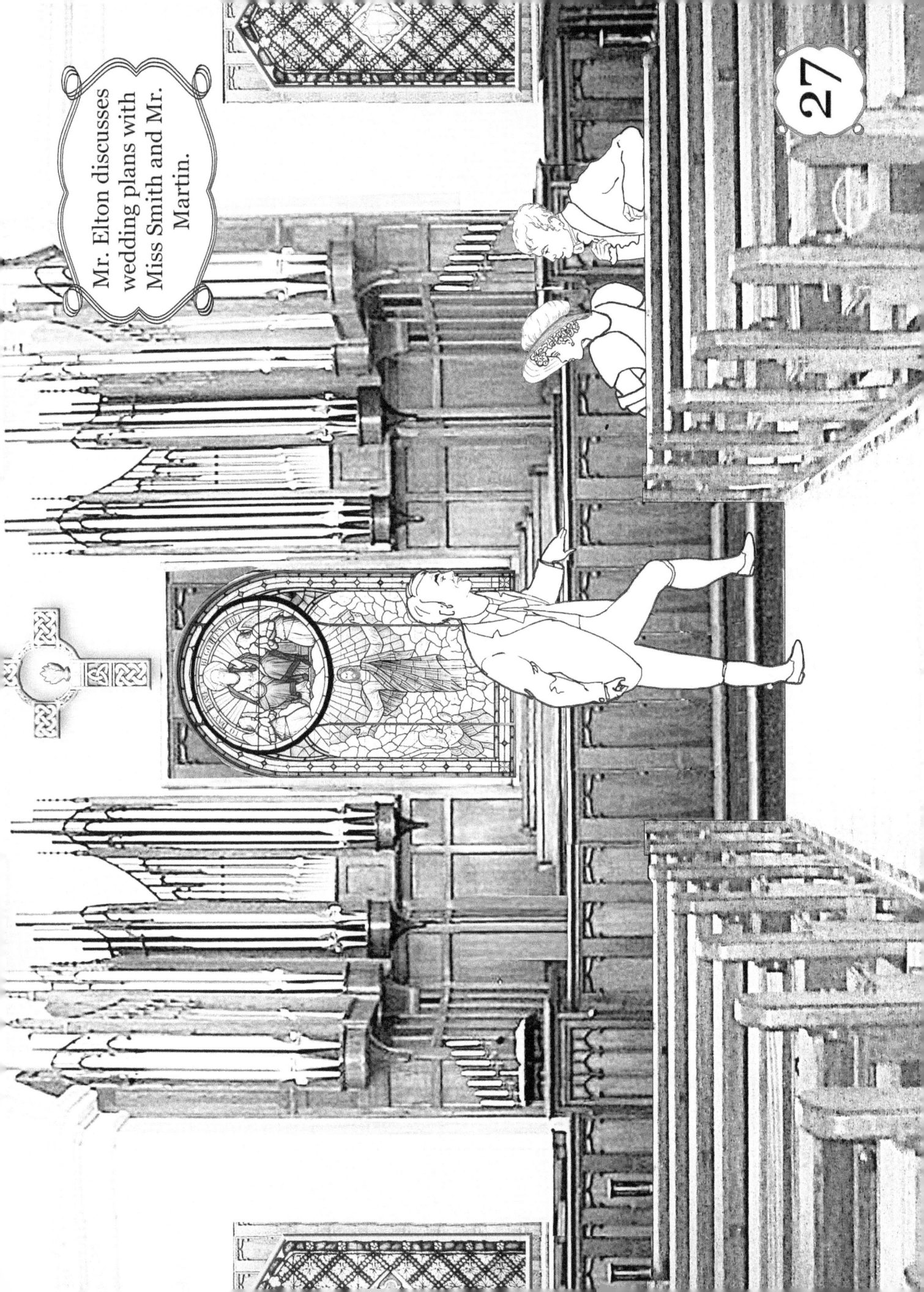

Mr. Elton discusses wedding plans with Miss Smith and Mr. Martin.

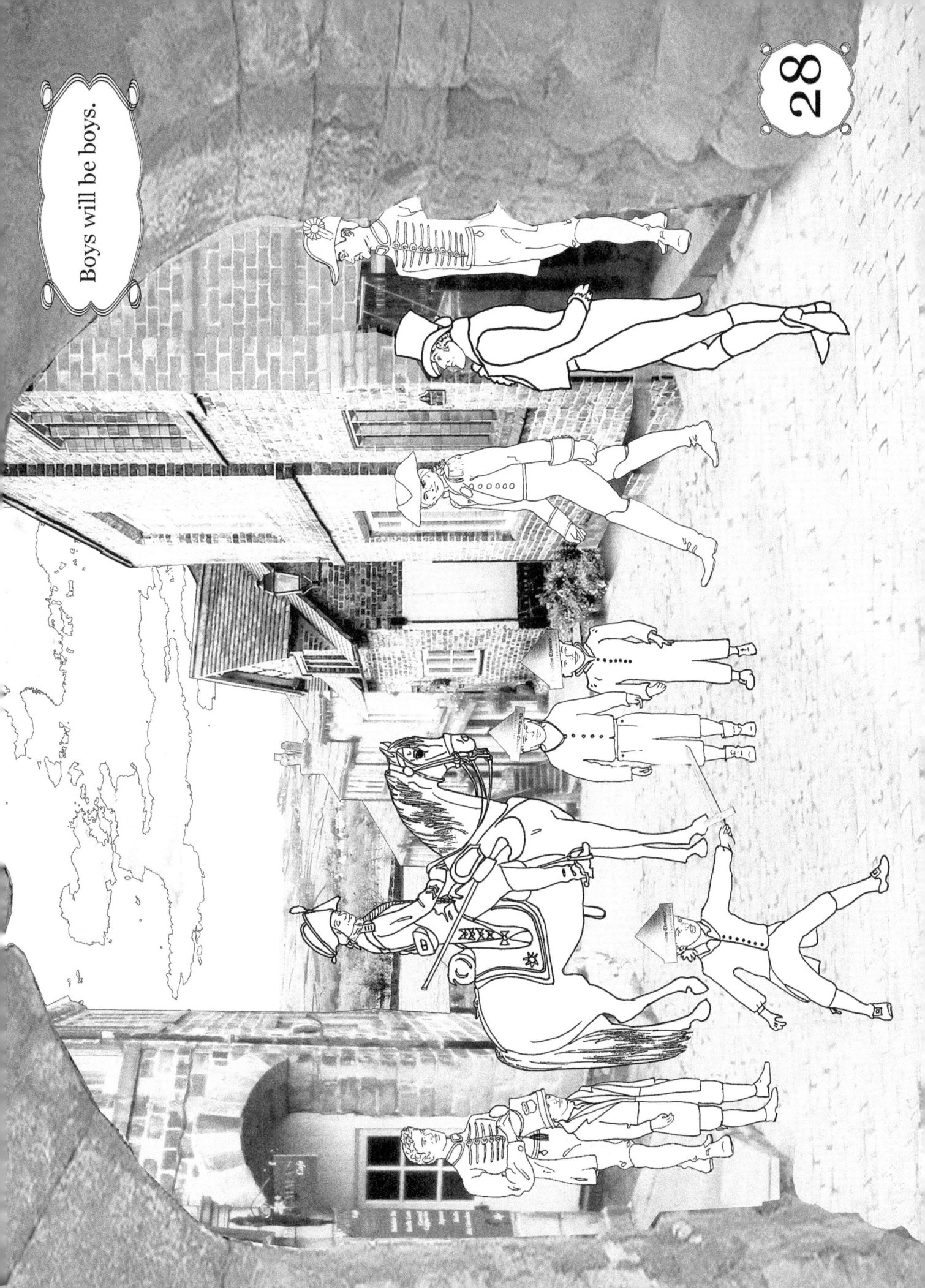

Boys will be boys.

28

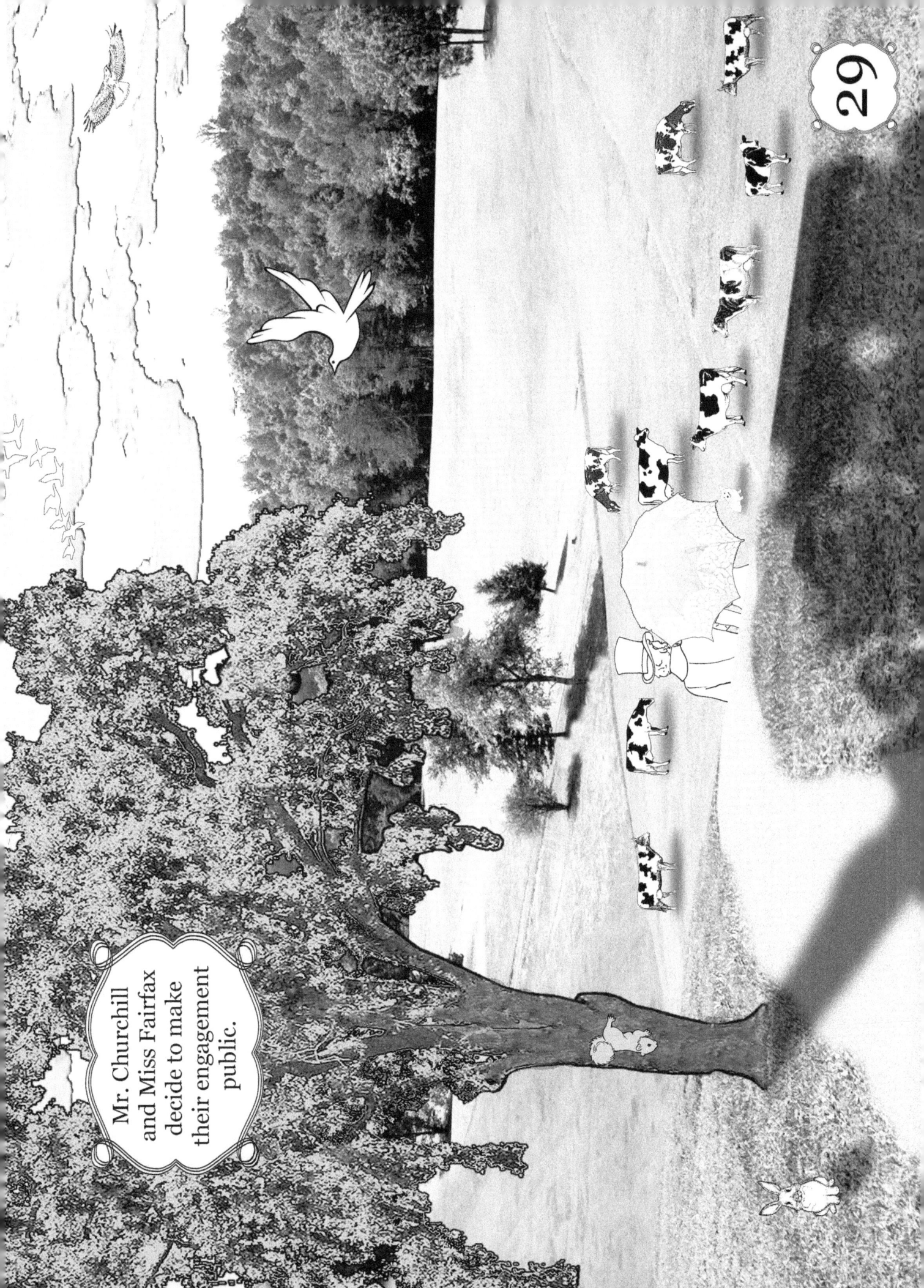

Mr. Churchill and Miss Fairfax decide to make their engagement public.

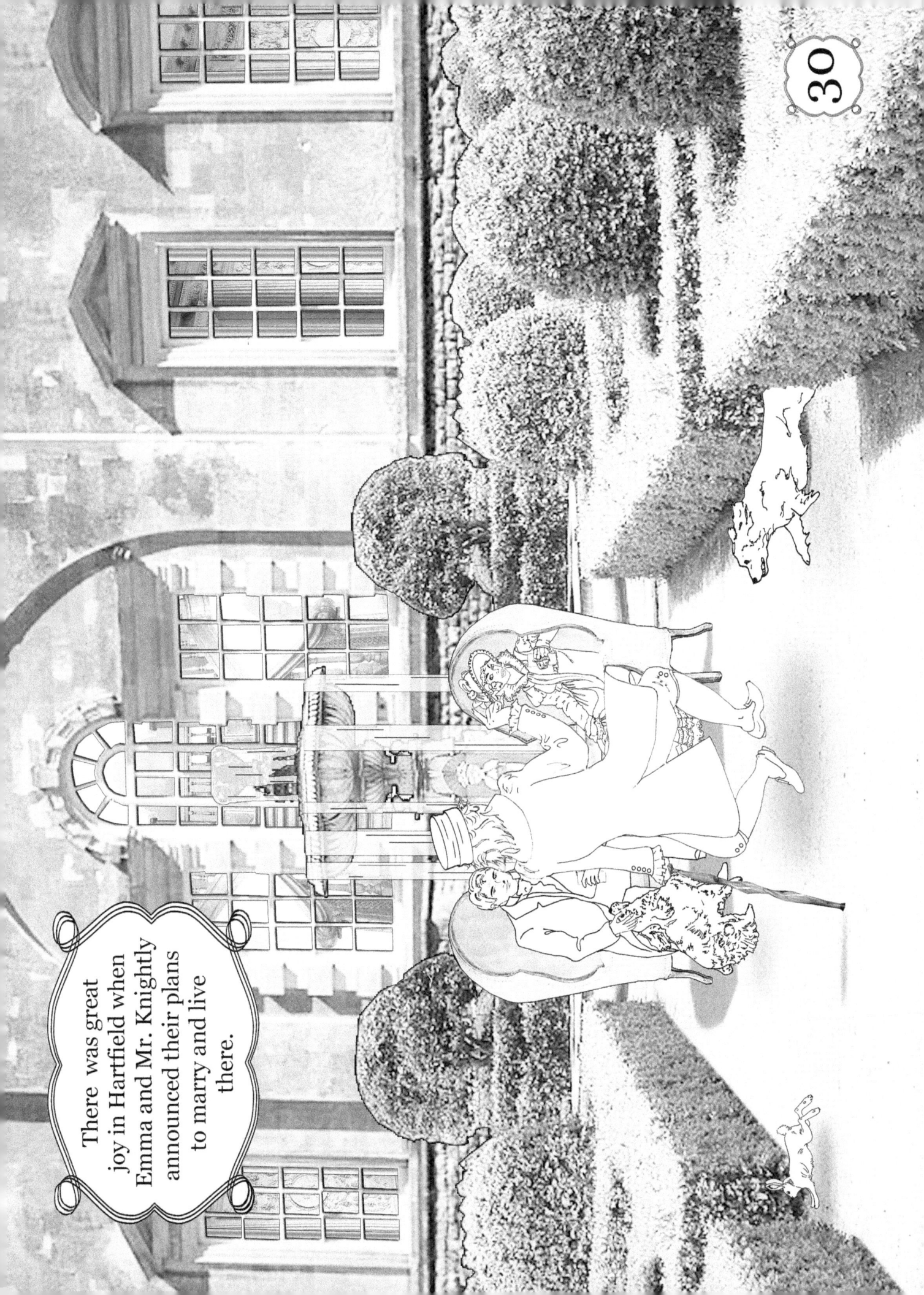

There was great joy in Hartfield when Emma and Mr. Knightly announced their plans to marry and live there.

www.ingramcontent.com/pod-product-compliance
Lightning Source LLC
Chambersburg PA
CBHW080630190526
45169CB00009B/3347